"THERE ARE HUMAN BODY PARTS ALL OVER!"

Deputy Sheriff Chris White walked slowly into the grassy field. The odor of death was overpowering. Drawn closer, he came upon a part of a skull, a scalp of blond hair, a leg bone, a foot bone, panties, and an upper torso of a young woman, clad in a ribbed knit tank top. A thick shoelace and a piece of fabric was twisted around what was left of her throat. He leaned over and almost gagged. A heart-shaped pendant necklace was still around her neck, and dark body fluids stained the ground under the decomposed body.

He'd seen enough.

The inhuman killer had claimed another victim.

BOUND TO DIE
ANNA FLOWERS

PINNACLE BOOKS
KENSINGTON PUBLISHING CORP.

PINNACLE BOOKS are published by

Kensington Publishing Corp.
850 Third Avenue
New York, NY 10022

Pinnacle and the P logo Reg. U.S. Pat. & TM Off.

First Printing: October, 1995

Printed in the United States of America

Thanks

To special agent Michael P. Malone, FBI, for introducing me to the hair and fiber labs in Washington, DC, through tours and slide briefing;

To the FBI Academy at Quantico, Virginia, who showed me around and gave me armfuls of helpful literature;

To Dr. Dennis Wickham, Brevard County medical examiner, who allowed me to stand next to him to study an autopsy;

To Chris Sabella, HCSO attorney, who gave me access to office public records and assisted me whenever possible;

To Det. Lee Baker, who personally opened many doors for me at HCSO;

To the Tampa Attorney General's Office;

To the Hillsborough County Clerk's Office;

To Ben Brotemarkle, National Public Radio, Orlando, Florida;

To my editor, Paul Dinas, and my agent, Nancy Love;

And to my family, for their help and patience.

Author's Note

This true account of the crimes of Bobby Joe Long is based on the voluminous Police Task Force Report, other police reports, audiotaped interviews, court records, and numerous newspaper articles and video accounts. Some names have been changed to protect the privacy of individuals connected to the case.

Foreword

This true crime story takes place in Tampa, Florida, which is part of a vast metropolitan area of over two million people. Situated in the latitudes of subtropic climate and growth, the area is lush with vegetation.

Violence has always been a part of Tampa's history. The original Indian population rebelled against Ponce de Leon in 1521, when he sailed his Spanish ships into Tampa Bay. Panfilo de Narvaez, a fiery one-eyed adventurer brought an expedition of 400 men into Tampa Bay in 1528. Although many died when supply ships did not return from Cuba, Cabeza de Vaca described Tampa as the best port in the world. Today, Tampa remains a major active port serving Florida and the southeastern United States.

Roguish pirates brought more violence to the coastline in the 1700s. The numerous coves made Florida prime for plunder. In 1763, Spain traded Florida to England for Havana. The name of Lord Hillsborough, the British colonial secretary of state in 1772, is still used for the county of which Tampa is the county seat, as well as the river and a bay. Florida became a territory of the United States in 1821, when Gen. Andrew Jackson became its first governor. Under military rule, Tampa began to flourish, and in 1824, Fort Brook was built. More violence came a decade later, with the Seminole War.

Florida became a state in 1845, and Tampa became incorporated ten years later. After a slow recovery from the Civil War, in 1885, the city began its transformation. Henry B. Plant had brought in his railroad the year before, providing the city with vital transportation. New industry began to grow with the discovery of phosphate pebbles, and city planners found ways to attract more business, even personally underwriting the purchase of land on which the first major industry, cigar manufacturing, was begun. Vincent Martinez Ybor, a native Spaniard and cigar manufacturer, moved to Tampa and created the cigar town of Ybor City. Attracted by good wages and plentiful work, Cubans and Sicilians came in large numbers.

The Hillsborough County Sheriff's Office building, which housed the task force that solved the Long case, is located in the center of Ybor City. The modern brick structure is surrounded by old cigar factories and Latin architecture.

Since the railroad first came to the port,

transportation systems have never stopped growing in Tampa. A complex system of bridges and interstate roads have made the city a transportation nucleus. Bobby Joe Long understood the highway system well and left most of his victims near major highways. Downtown Tampa, like many other large cities that expanded outward, has an abundance of bars and pornographic establishments. Bars and abandoned buildings became convenient sites for drug traffic. The gaudy "Strip" in Tampa is a small area along Nebraska Avenue north of Kennedy Boulevard where, especially during the 1980s, crime, prostitution, and cocaine sales ran rampant.

As Long was working this neon beat picking up girls in his car and murdering them, crack cocaine was sweeping the city. Robberies almost doubled as users tried to support their addiction and murders increased by over fifty percent. Women openly prostituted themselves for drug money. When a recent national television program depicted the extent of America's drug problem, its producers chose Tampa for the film's locale.

A variety of illicit activity has plagued Tampa throughout this century, but few periods were as chilling as the six-month reign of terror in 1984, when fear of a serial killer gripped the city.

One

"Look at it fly!" Two seventeen-year-old boys tossed homemade plastic bag parachutes toward the sky in a cow pasture near I-75, southeast of Tampa, Florida. Their peals of laughter floated across the field on this picture-perfect afternoon. It was Mother's Day, May 13, 1984. Retrieving one chute, which had floated down to rest on what appeared to be a dead animal, they were horrified to discover the maggot-infested body of a nude young woman. Repressing the urge to vomit, they ran to call the Hillsborough County Sheriff's Office.

Capt. Gary Terry and Det. Lee Baker were the first to arrive at the crime scene. For a few moments they stared in amazement at the body. The woman lay on her stomach, her legs forced apart wider than she was tall. Some inhuman creature had pounded her severely and lashed her wrists behind her back with knotted rope. A cumbersome noose had been looped three times around her neck and tied with still another kind of rope. She looked monstrously like a roped and tied calf that had been mangled and left in the field.

"My God, she took a beating." Terry shuddered as he got a deep whiff of the decomposing body. In the Florida heat, dead bodies do not last long. Although he was middle-aged, Terry had a boyish appearance, with straight brown hair spilling across his forehead. His large eyes were weary from looking at dead girls, and they were the only feature that betrayed his true age. "What'ya think?" he asked Baker. "About three days on this one?"

Baker nodded, his index finger automatically pushing his wire-rimmed glasses up on his nose. He had a pleasant presence that projected a kind of fatherly trust. Graying hair topped his amiable face. People called him "Pops."

"He must have broken both her hips to pull her legs that far apart," he sighed. Her legs were pulled at right angles to her petite body. Her jet-black hair was about the only part of her left intact. "Probably Asian," he guessed.

Terry's brow wrinkled as his sharp eyes studied the small figure. "You can almost sense the creep that did this," he muttered, as other technicians began to gather at the scene.

In fact, the killer had left his imprint with

tire tracks starting at a barricade that blocked the dirt access road to the field. The barricade was part of the construction area control for the I-75 complex construction equipment. He had driven about 300 feet into the field where the attack had occurred. Afterward he had backed up his car about forty feet before swinging around to head past the barricade again. He came within three feet of the fence to scurry past the barricade on the same side where he'd entered.

Plaster tire impressions were made of this by Technician Daniel McGill, while Judy Swann started taking photographs. This tire evidence would become invaluable. The front and rear right tires had the same standard tread design as most manufacturers used, but the left rear tire was unusual.

"Can I get to her now?" asked Dr. Charles Digg, the deputy medical examiner. Terry waved his slender hand with the large class ring and nodded. The doctor kneeled to examine more carefully the rope around the victim's neck and looked up wide-eyed. "This is absolutely bizarre!"

Her anguished face had plowed the ground as she had been ridden from behind, arms tied behind her back; a restraining rope around her neck had been jerked as she was being raped and strangled to death. The men studied the physical evidence that gave witness to this horrible death.

Dr. Digg grunted as Baker leaned forward to look closely at the white silk cloth under her head. "Could have been used as a gag," the detective said.

Terry was having another thought. Over thirty bodies had been found so far this year in Hillsborough County, but this one was very unique, ghoulishly sexual, almost staged.

Finally, he spoke to Baker, squinting his eyes in a gesture that lined his forehead. "I think we'd better call the FBI in on this one," he said quietly. Almost immediately, these veteran law enforcement officers knew that they had a deranged killer on the loose.

The body had been reported late in the day and the investigating team was happy that the limited amount of evidence allowed them to wrap up the case quickly. Everything was photographed. The scarf, ropes, and tire imprints were all plotted on a chart, then marked, boxed, and returned to the HCSO.

As the body was being prepared for transport to his office, Dr. Digg pondered the kind of person whose handiwork would produce such a tortured corpse. Although he had been in this business for many years, the depth of human cruelty still amazed and saddened him.

Once back at his office, Dr. Digg donned his green surgical scrubs, shoe covers, mask, and hat. He immediately started to work taking X-rays. No projectiles showed up in the body and there were no stab wounds.

Dep. Arthur Pickard and Technician Racey Wilson photographed the body and took fingerprints from the left hand. Dr. Digg noted that the woman weighed eighty-eight pounds, measured five feet, two inches, and had small breasts and shoulder-length black hair. Samples of pubic and cranial hair were collected, as were fingernail clippings. Oral, anal, and vaginal swabbings were collected.

Dr. Digg removed the ligatures intact from the victim's wrists by slipping the rope and cloth over her hands. Pickard placed these items in a paper bag while Digg cut the rope from around the woman's neck. The knot area was near the front of the throat, so a cut was made to the left of the knot. The ends of the rope were then color-coded with tape and removed from around the neck. The ends were taped together and the rope was put into an evidence bag, and photographs were taken of the ligature marks on the wrists and neck.

The doctor opened the torso cavity and collected blood and urine samples. He noted that the stomach was empty and the victim was not pregnant. He examined the neck area and found bruising where the ropes had been, but the hyoid bone was intact. His conclusion was that the cause of death had been strangulation.

* * *

At four o'clock the same day, Capt. Terry called special agent Michael P. Malone at the FBI lab in Washington, DC. Malone settled his large frame comfortably in his chair and listened intently to Terry's details of the case. His intelligence was evident in his wide face. His large brown eyes narrowed as he instantly absorbed the information he was hearing. Malone was good. In just eight years he had become recognized as a top forensic expert whose hair and fiber analysis was legendary. He respected professional performance in the field and he was pleased to be getting it now.

"Bring me what you've got," he said, when Terry was finished talking. He hesitated a moment to soften his next request, "And I'll also need her hands."

Immediately, Det. Baker was flown to Washington with the evidence. This now included the hands, which had been surgically removed from the victim by the authorities and put in separate plastic containers. The ropes, the white scarf, and the tire castings were packaged carefully as well.

Baker rode straight from National Airport along Potomac River Drive, turned before he got to the Pentagon, and went across the 16th Street Bridge, which channels incoming traffic into downtown Washington.

The FBI Hoover Building has very high

concrete steps that extend the entire width of the vast old building. From street level, it is almost like a palace fortress— strong, and seemingly not easily penetrated. Baker's nostrils were filled with the scent of Asian street cooking, and an earlier spring shower had put a slight chill in the air. There was nothing about the building that looked particularly American. It could have been in the center of any city in the world. It was as Hoover must have intended it to be: authoritative, removed from people, and intimidating.

Baker proceeded down the ramp to the underground lobby, where he would have easier access with his packages. He registered with Security, was issued a visitor's badge, and waited for his escort, who would take him down the hall to the elevators and up to the third floor where Malone waited.

The hair and fiber unit is entered through a small hall from the main corridor. Baker entered the main room, about thirty feet square, which had many tables packed with boxes of labeled case materials. Baker set his parcels down with the rest as Malone entered from his office and the two exchanged greetings.

There were small briefing rooms, individual office/laboratories, and scraping rooms off the main room. As he talked about the case, Baker noticed the unusual items used

as weapons in other cases, such as bowling
pins and yard tools.

The evidence was soon taken into an adjoining scraping room. These were three
separate glass-enclosed rooms with controlled
environment and temperature. In the middle
of each room was a large four-by-six-foot table above which hung a rack similar to a
clothesline. Here the items were suspended
from a rod above the table and brushed with
a stainless steel spatula. Hair and fiber samples fell onto the sterile paper on the table-
top and were collected for microanalysis.

Baker wanted to keep an accurate diary of
facts, and with Malone's patient help, the
equipment being used was systematically
identified for him. For the fiber examinations
a stereoscopic microscope, a comparison microscope, a polarized light microscope, a mi-
crospectrophotometer, a melting-point
apparatus, and eventually, an infrared spec-
trophotometer were used. With this equipment, the lab could compare and identify the
smallest shred of evidence. Baker had to return to Florida, but the Hillsborough County
Sheriff's Office would hear from Malone
soon.

Meanwhile, legwork continued as HCSO
interviewed John Corcoran, who had filed a
missing persons report on a woman fitting

the victim's description. He'd brought in information about the woman and some photographs of her. Clearly recalling the corpse they had just seen at the medical examiner's office, the detectives felt fairly certain that she was John's friend, Ngeun Thi Long, or Lana Long.

John signed a consent form for search of his apartment. Det. King contacted Technician Wilson at his home to bring the prints, taken at the autopsy, to the apartment in the Shadow Oaks subdivision. This second-floor flat was a modest one-bedroom, one-bath apartment.

Wilson lifted latent fingerprints from a drinking glass, metal box, and perfume bottle. With these prints, the identification of Lana Long was definite. They then contacted Terry and coordinated all the known information.

Lana Long was a twenty-year-old Laotian who had come to the United States ten years earlier with her family to live in Los Angeles. While performing as a go-go dancer there, she had met John. Although he was older, about thirty-five, Lana had liked him enough to move to Tampa with him when he'd gotten a job with a motion picture company there. They'd set up housekeeping at Shadow Oaks, but after a few months she had become bored and decided to start dancing again. She took a part-time job at the Sly Fox Lounge on the Strip on Nebraska Avenue.

"She was bubbly," said Sly Fox owner Lamar Golden. "A really fun girl. I think her biggest problem was a drug addiction. She didn't have a car, either, and she was forever trying to get rides."

Lana was unreliable about coming to work, but normally she worked the night shift until closing. She had a habit of telling customers that she would go out with them later so they would buy her drinks, but she usually found a reason not to go. She liked to drink and also used cocaine and other drugs if she could get them. Sometimes she would go to other bars with customers after work.

The last place she was seen in public was leaving a bar and restaurant called CC's, located on Fletcher, near Nebraska. The place was a favorite hangout where she routinely sat at the bar with a drink and watched the action. The bartender recalled that she was a petite and pretty girl who wore a lot of jewelry and that she had a very appealing personality.

Just a few weeks before her death, Lana had quit her job and told friends that she planned to study art at the University of South Florida. Her apartment was near USF, where there were many transients and small businesses. A witness reported seeing her at her apartment, just before her disappearance, wearing shorts and a tank top.

Unlike many of the four thousand Tampa Bay-area residents of Southeast Asian descent, Long apparently did not maintain ties to the community.

"I don't think any family in this area will know her," said Ngu Do, a state worker who herself had strong ties to the Asian community. "Work and school is where I send our young people," she said. "No dancing!"

Gary Terry and his staff at HCSO were frustrated with the lack of leads and additional evidence. They knew a lot about Lana Long, but nothing about her killer. Every possible lead was followed, every phone tip checked out. They were only deadends. Finally, the FBI lab report came from Mike Malone.

Hair evidence that had been removed was either the victim's hair or "unsuitable for comparison." The serology examinations were also negative, due to the decomposition of the body. The ropes and knots used to bind the victim were identified, but they revealed little. The casts of the tire treads proved interesting and definitely had potential future use, but for the present, they were filed. However, in examining the fibers, Malone discovered the first important lead in the case. From the scarf he found a single lustrous red trilobal nylon fiber. The size, type, and cross-sectional shape of the fiber indicated that this was from carpet, probably of the type used in an automobile, perhaps that of the killer.

Since Lana had been found in a remote area, she had most likely been transported in a vehicle, and the carpeting of this vehicle was probably the last she had come in contact with. The killer was probably driving a car with red carpet. This report was forwarded to HCSO with the caution that the fiber information should be kept confidential. As with the case of Wayne Williams, the convicted Atlanta serial killer of black boys, police didn't want the murderer alerted and changing his killing pattern or his car. All that HCSO could release to the media was that they'd found a body and that it had been identified as that of Lana Long.

Two

The media had more to work with two weeks later on May 27, when the brutally murdered body of a beautiful twenty-two year-old woman was found. They quickly published a composite drawing of her and told how she had been found twelve hours after her gruesome death off Park Road just north of I-4 at Plant City in a lover's lane. She was quickly identified as Michelle Denise Simms, a former California beauty contestant who more recently had worked as a hooker to support a drug habit.

A burly construction worker had found her, and the startling scene had made him weep. She was lying nude on her back, her cheeks and neck caked with dried blood from a knife slashing. A rope was wound around her neck and her arms were tied at the wrists and secured around her body. All she wore were an ankle bracelet and round pierced earrings.

When Capt. Bill Miller, Capt. Terry, and Sgt. Randy Latimer arrived at the crime scene,

Technician Don Hunt and medical examiner Lee Miller were arriving as well. The scene was ghastly, with blood everywhere. A blood-stained white jumpsuit and a pair of bloody white pantyhose were hanging from a tree limb. A breeze animated the pantyhose so they beckoned the men with ghostly waving legs. There was an eerie feeling that a monster had been here the night before and his presence was felt even now.

A long-ended ligature secured in a hangman's slip knot had been wrapped around the woman's neck three times. This had been partially severed, apparently by one of the knife slashes to the neck. A green T-shirt bound her upper arms. The shirt seemed to have been ripped or cut up the front and pulled down across the victim's back with both arms still in their sleeves. Her throat had been slashed several times deeply enough to sever a large blood vessel and cause death.

Soon other detectives arrived, and to a man, they investigated almost silently. This was not the sort of homicide scene they had steeled themselves against; this was a slaughter. The smell of death hung in the air.

Baker took a deep breath and drew nearer the body. He found what appeared to be a reddish fiber on the victim near her left breast, and there were several strands of hair on her lower stomach and under her right hand. Hunt collected samples of the fiber and hair and also took into evidence a fresh Michelob bottle that lay near her feet. Had the monster taken time for a beer?

There was a dirt road in the field running west off Park Street that passed about eight feet from the body. Here they found the print of a bare foot and also several tire track impressions in the dirt. The tracks seemed to have been caused by a vehicle turning around in the area near the body. The footprint was cast, and seven cast impressions were made of the tire tracks. This evidence was again quickly sent to the FBI lab. Terry and Baker strongly believed, as did other homicide detectives, that the murders of Michelle Simms and Lana Long were related.

The stainless steel gurney was pushed into position near the sink in the Hillsborough County medical examiner's lab. Dr. Lee Miller was about to start the autopsy on Michelle Simms. Lee Baker, Hawkins, and Hunt all gazed at the victim, lying much as she had been found, with throat slashed and neck and arms bound. Since the body was only twelve hours old, Dr. Miller expected it to reveal a lot. He wasn't disappointed.

The rope used in the hangman's slip knot was different from the clothesline cord used to secure her wrists. This was tied in single loops around each wrist and across the front and back of the body, and it was secured by a granny knot across the left front of the abdomen.

Continuing the external examination, Dr. Miller noted that the teeth were natural and in good repair. The fingernails were short and there were no injuries of the hands or foreign material there, except for a small amount of dirt and some blood splatters. Remnants of peach nail lacquer were present on the toenails. The tanning pattern of a bikini with high-cut thighs was present. The lateral edges of the pubic hair had been shaved, showing a slight stubble of regrowth. The external and internal aspects of the genitalia and anus were unremarkable, but the vagina contained a small amount of pasty white fluid.

The cranial hair was dark brown, straight, and styled to medium length. Miller cut her hair in back precisely at the neckline and pulled the scalp over the face for access to the cranium. A saw cut the bone at the base of the skull and the brain was removed. The cranial bones were intact. There was moderately extensive hemorrhaging. The skull had received five heavy blows. There was a one-inch-by-two-inch area of reddish-purple contusions on the lateral left temporal lobe, but it did not extend to the white matter.

There were also massive injuries to the muscle of the neck overlying the voicebox and the skin of the neck. This, together with pinpoint hemorrhages of the whites of her eyes, indicated that the victim had been strangled at or near the point of death.

The chest was opened through the usual incision, and the small amount of blood removed was put in a tube. Interior organs were individually removed, weighed, and cataloged. A small piece of each was sliced and kept as a specimen. The remaining portion of the lungs, heart, liver, kidney, and brain were put in a large stainless steel bowl. When the autopsy was complete, the organs were dumped from the bowl into a plastic bag that was placed back into the body cavity and the body was sewn up. The hair was pulled from the face back to its original place over the cranium and the body looked much the same as it had when it was rolled in.

The official cause of death was reported to be asphyxiation and closed head injuries.

In their investigation of Simms, HCSO found that she had been in Tampa only one night before her murder. She was originally from California but had left there in 1980 with Tom Sanchez to live in Fort Pierce, Florida. They were together for about three years. According to Sanchez, Michelle was addicted to cocaine.

"[Michelle] was going through about one thousand [dollars] a week for cocaine," he reported, "since she was getting into freebasing. I was trying to get her to quit. It was ruining her life." But she refused to even try to quit or to help herself. They parted in December of 1983, six months before her murder.

On her own again, she started working as a prostitute. On the night of her murder, she was last seen talking to two white men near Kennedy Boulevard.

Michelle had an aunt and uncle who had raised her in rural Cutler, California, from the age of three. Prison officials verified that the father had been incarcerated from 1966 to 1977, after which he had disappeared. While her father was in prison, Michelle's mother had died, leaving her without any immediate family.

"She was a very confused girl and didn't know what she wanted from day to day," her aunt recalled. "She called me for silly things. Once she called to see if I had got an eight-cent postcard from North Carolina. She was very loving but very confused. We did the best we could for her. For her to end up like this just isn't fair." She lowered her

head to her hand and added, "A beautiful
girl was brutally murdered, and I think people should focus on that."

Three

Back at the FBI lab in Washington, Mike Malone was encouraged. His hard work, combined with luck, was paying off. His rarely used, but engaging, smile spread across his face. The tire impressions found near Simms matched those found at the Long murder scene. One of the impressions from the right rear was identified as a Goodyear Viva tire, which had the whitewall facing inward. When the left rear tire could not be identified, HCSO contacted an expert in Akron, Ohio. The casts were flown there and were identified as a "Vogue Tyre," an expensive tire that comes only on Cadillacs.

Also a match to the Lana Long evidence was a lustrous red trilobal nylon fiber. A second type, a delustered red trilobal fiber, was found, indicating that the killer was driving a vehicle containing two different types of carpet fibers.

Semen stains from Michelle's clothing were tested and found to disclose the presence of both A and B blood group substances. Eight-inch brown Caucasian cranial hairs which could have been those of the killer were found on her body. With this information, HCSO went to work building a physical evidence profile of the two-victim killer. This data was distributed to other law enforcement agencies.

The murderer had been methodical. He had prepared himself by having an ample supply of rope or cord, cut to lengths appropriate for his intended use of tying and immobilizing his victim, and he had armed himself with a hunting knife. With these preparations made, he went in search of a victim, who'd chanced to be Michelle Simms. Inviting her into his car in a cold, calculated, and obviously premeditated manner, he stripped her and bound her with rope prepared for this very purpose. Without any human regard for her, he brutally raped her. Finally, he took her to another location, and there he strangled her, bludgeoned her, and eventually slashed her throat.

HCSO sent an explicit summary of known common factors on the two Tampa Bay murders to the FBI, stating similarities in the two cases.

The Behavioral Science Services Unit of the FBI is located at the FBI Academy in Quantico, Virginia. It is contained in an underground facility built by J. Edgar Hoover, former FBI director, as a bomb shelter during World War II. The mission of the BSSU is to develop and provide programs of training, consultation, and information in the behavioral and social sciences for the law enforcement community that will help improve their effectiveness.

In the Criminal Investigative Analysis Subunit, profiles of unknown offenders are constructed through a detailed analysis of violent crimes and aberrant behavior. In addition, consultation is provided that may include investigative strategy, interviewing and proactive investigative techniques, search warrant information, personality assessments, and prosecution strategy. Special agent crime analysts are available for on-site major case analysis and consultation with law enforcement officials involved with major violent crime investigations.

After they received the information from HCSO, the Criminal Investigative Analysis Subunit prepared a detailed projected killer profile. They deduced that both Long and Simms had been randomly selected as targets by the killer. Their respective life-styles placed them in positions where they were susceptible to approach, and the killer most likely would have presumed the victims would not be reported missing for some time.

The following factors, as related by the HCSO, were considered especially important in connection with the preparation of this profile. Both victims had to depend upon someone else for transportation, and they were both completely nude at the time their bodies were discovered. Also significant was the fact that both were tied in a somewhat similar manner; and in the case of Long, the body seemed to have been displayed somewhat symbolically. Both victims were found in relatively close proximity to interstate highways in rural areas of Hillsborough County after having been abducted in more urban sections of Tampa.

The fact that Long and Simms were found some distance from the location of their actual abductions is also significant in that this factor demonstrates the mobility of the murderer. The fact that Simms was cut and beaten beyond the degree necessary to accomplish her murder indicates a motive on the part of the perpetrator beyond that of simple homicide. Also, the ropes found around the necks of each of the victims with leashlike leaders demonstrates a deviant personality trait in the murderer. The carpet fibers found on both bodies which have been identified by the FBI Laboratory confirms the relationship between the two homicides even beyond that demonstrated by similar personality traits as evidenced in the respective crime scene analyses.

The perpetrator would probably not have known his victims, and they were randomly selected, as evidenced by the fact that their respective life-styles made them easy prey.

Personality Characteristics

The killer is probably white, in his mid-twenties and is most likely to be a gregarious individual who is an extrovert and manipulative of others. He operates normally within society and seems to adjust well to a variety of circumstances. He is an argumentative individual who does not keep his anger inside but who vents his emotions, thereby frequently getting into arguments and fights. He is in all likelihood self-centered and selfish and exhibits little or no emotion. He is generally not a team player; and if he is on a team, he feels he must be the center of attention. He is most likely an impulsive individual, though this impulsiveness is tempered with sufficient judgment that he would not take chances when committing a crime, and therefore would be difficult to identify. Probabilities are that the subject is a pathological liar who would make a good hired tough or strong-arm man. This individual feels he must be the leader of the pack, and *he has strong identification with his macho image. Frequently, he will be found to have one or more tattoos exhibiting the more masculine aspects of his personality. The killer may also be a police buff, and he may be inclined to carry a weapon if he feels he can get away with it.*

Education

He will probably be high-school educated at best. If he did get to college, he would be the type of individual who would have difficulty adjusting to the discipline and would probably drop out. He might have the intellectual potential to achieve well in a university setting. However, his lack of discipline and his resentment of authority would be prime factors in causing him to drop out. His marginal performance in high school would primarily be due to lack of application, and he would likely have been disruptive in class. He might have been a truant. If he had ever been assigned to remedial classes, this situation would have resulted from his emotional immaturity rather than any lack of intellectual ability to grasp the material. He would most likely hang around a high school after dropping out. He would obtain employment in a traditionally masculine job, such as truck driver or mechanic.

As he matures, he would have a tendency to gravitate toward sales or some type of occupation where his manipulative skills could be most effectively utilized. He probably has had difficulty holding down a job for any period of time and his history will most likely demonstrate multiple employments lasting only 90 to 100 days.

Childhood Characteristics

The subject would most likely have been considered to be a delinquent during his youth who was difficult to control and who resented parental or any other type of discipline. A history of bedwetting, arson, and animal torture would most likely be evident.

Military

If he joined the service, he would most likely be found in one of the most masculine branches, such as the Marine Corps, or in some type of specialized Army training. Given his history of being unable to stand criticism, it is likely that he would have gotten into trouble after only a few months in the service caused by his retaliating against discipline.

Social Life

This type of person will generally have a woman in his life. He dates regularly but not steadily for any long period of time. His female associates would normally be younger, and he would be inclined to discard women after sexual conquest. He likes to boast of his exploits and impress the people he comes in contact with, regardless of gender. If married, he would most likely be an unfaithful husband with a dependent wife. He is the type of person who would tire of a long-term marriage commitment and frequently his marriage would end in divorce.

Habit

The subject probably purchased an automobile as soon as possible in order to allow him the mobility he desires. He loves to drive. If he could afford it, he would most likely own a flashy sports car. He identifies with his vehicle.

Criminal History

This person might have begun his criminal career committing neighborhood crimes, which would have been expanded to more *distant areas once he was able to achieve mobility. He is carrying a weapon. If he has ever spent time in prison, he might be a model prisoner, quite capable of manipulating prison guard personnel as well as other prisoners.*

Habits Related to Present Crime

He would have most likely used a ruse to gain control of his victim and he would be inclined to torture her mentally. Given the trauma exhibited on the body of Simms and the fact that both she and Long had ropes tied around their necks, there is a strong indication that in this particular case, the torture was physical in addition to mental. He kept her alive for some period of time in order to taunt her. He would generally leave little or no evidence behind. As noted above, the murderer was probably not familiar with his victims. However, if he had been acquainted with them, there would most likely be indications of facial disfiguration in order to dehumanize his victims. This particular subject would be likely to kill again, typically in serial fashion. He might confine his activity to a given geographic region but would be quite capable of traveling to other areas of the state or country to murder.

Post-Offense Behavior

This type of individual returns to the scene of his crime and injects himself into the investigations of law enforcement authorities. This action on his part would accomplish two ends. First, he achieves a high by reliving the experience of the homicide itself. Second, he volunteers information to officials to mislead them in identifying the perpetrator. He might also contact the family of the victim, the media, or police officials on certain anniversary dates. He would most likely continue the same life-style after the crime as that he lived prior to it. He would do little to draw attention to himself and therefore would probably not change jobs or his social life after the crime.

Interview Techniques

It would probably be most effective to use direct interviewing techniques in questioning him. The interviewer should know the murder cold and direct the questioning from a position of strength, since the only thing the subject would respect would be confidence. The interviewer should be nonchalant, thereby maintaining control of the interview, and he should be totally familiar with significant dates in the background of the mur-

derer, dropping such information in a timed fashion throughout the interview in order to give the interviewee the impression that his entire background is known to authorities. The interviewer may wish to reinforce his position of authority by dressing formally and creating an environment wherein he is viewed by the subject as a totally professional and confident law enforcement officer who is in a position of authority over those around him.

By the time this report arrived in Florida, HCSO had more murders on their hands.

Four

A quiet young woman with a different life-style from that of the bawdy streetwalkers disappeared two weeks after the Simms murder. Elizabeth Loudenback, 22, lived just east of notorious Nebraska Avenue in the Village Mobile Home Park on Skipper Road. The cruising killer must have found her easy prey.

She lived in a trailer with her mother, stepfather, brother, and sister. Probably because of the lack of space, she liked to walk a lot, but she usually stayed close to home. Each day she rode to work, with her mother, to Odessa, where she worked on the assembly line as a solderer in an electronics factory. She was very shy, wore glasses, and had straight reddish hair cut in long bangs. She was epileptic and took antiseizure medication three times a day.

Neighbors characterized her as a loner who would sit by herself at the community pool and read a book. Sometimes, however, she and a male friend would walk across the street to Grampa's Pool Parlor, where she would have a beer and watch him shoot pool.

On June 8, after work, she took her paycheck to the bank with her mother. Later, she walked out the front entrance of the mobile park and was never seen again. That night, as she walked hurriedly along, she found herself on Nebraska Avenue, about a block north of Fletcher, where an attractive man in a good-looking car pulled up alongside her and asked her if she wanted a ride.

"All right," she said with uncharacteristic pluck, "but just don't try anything."

The man smiled, and as soon as she was in the car, he pulled a knife from under the seat. She screamed and cried, but he slapped her and warned her to be quiet. Even though she obeyed, he hit her again as he was tying her hands. She shuddered when he pulled down her jeans and forced her to take them off. He made her lie facedown on the reclined seat and tied her arms behind her and then raped her from behind.

He sped off and drove until he came to an orange grove in Brandon, where he drove back deep among the trees. It was very dark when he stopped the car. He ferociously raped her again. When he was finished, he allowed her to pull her pants back on. He ignored her whimpering, warning her to be silent. He made her bounds tighter before he pushed her out of the car. Once out, he grabbed a piece of rope and strangled her to death. He threw her body into some shrubs, then paused to bend over to scoop up her purse. On second thought, he decided to take the ropes as well.

Riding along with the window down and the wind blowing through his thick brown hair, he sneered and rifled through the purse on the seat where Elizabeth had sat. He found an automatic bank teller card and, unbelievably, the four-digit access number in a small envelope. In the next few hours, he used the card in rapid succession to obtain money from several banks. When he was finished with it, as he had done with the girl, he just threw the card away.

A few days after her disappearance, Elizabeth's frantic mother reported her missing, stating that a two-day supply of medicine which she carried would now have run out. The rest of her medication and her clothes had been left at home. But the police could find no leads in their investigation. They talked to her employer and co-workers and to neighbors, who all agreed that she probably would not get into a car with a stranger. It was as though she had disappeared into thin air.

When her body was finally found, sixteen

days after her murder, it was badly decomposed. The skeletal remains had maggots devouring most of it. On the bones were blue and white TRAX athletic shoes, blue jeans, and a green tube top. The head was turned to the left, with the arms extending outward. A gold pierced earring and a yellow-gold necklace with a floating heart-shaped amulet were still in place. The ground was stained with body fluids beneath her that continued in a stream downhill for about five feet. Her pockets were empty and no purse was found.

Photographs were taken and her clothing was removed by the medical examiner to be analyzed by the FBI. The corpse weighed only twenty-five pounds, and the hyoid bone had been broken during her strangulation. But there had been no ropes present this time and the victim had not been found nude near an interstate, as in the previous two homicides. The evidence was forwarded to the FBI lab anyway, but no request was made to compare it with that from the Long and Simms murders.

At first the FBI did a routine check of hairs and some serology examinations, but all were negative due to the advanced decomposition of the body. Much later, however, they were asked to examine the clothes for fiber evidence, and the same two types of red carpet fibers were found as had been found in the Simms and Long homicides. If this had been done initially, Loudenback would have been immediately identified as the third victim of a Tampa Bay serial killer.

For the time being, this victim was not tied to the other two due to an apparent lack of similarity. Different FBI lab technicians had worked on this case. In the investigation of serial murders, it is essential to have the same crime scene technicians and forensic detectives conduct studies of evidence from all the cases. Only then can patterns be established and linked to one individual killer.

Sheriff Walter Heinrich's Office (HCSO) was getting increasing pressure from the press. All they could say was, "A preliminary autopsy report has been completed, but the Sheriff's Department is not releasing the findings."

Obvious evidence had misled police in this investigation. The victim was completely different from the others in appearance, habits, and life-style. The death scene was completely different. No ropes were present. The victim was fully clothed, and she was not found near an interstate highway.

During the early investigation, the victim's boyfriend appeared to be a strong suspect in the murder after he failed a polygraph examination. Subsequent questioning and investigation cleared him, but for the time being, Loudenback was still not included as one of the serial killings.

Five

"Hey, whore, move it!" The blaring horn and obnoxious voice faded into the night. Chanel Williams jumped away from the road, startled. She was still not used to her new profession. She was eighteen years old, athletic, with long legs. Tonight her yellow blouse complemented her brown skin. She had left her hometown of nearby Bartow only a few weeks before. Even though it was right down the highway, the small-town atmosphere of sleepy Bartow seemed a million miles away from the honky-tonk Strip in Tampa where Chanel now strolled. It was September 30, 1984.

Chanel had just been released from jail two days earlier after an arrest for prostitution. Although her mother did not know that Chanel had chosen the easy-money but hard life of prostitution, before too long she was bound to find out. Chanel would have liked to please her mother, but somehow she had gotten off track. As a teenager, Chanel had been sent to a girls' reformatory for helping a friend steal a television set. Although she'd earned her high school equivalency degree there, she was basically untrained. Chanel didn't want a job serving fast food, but she wanted the things that money can buy. Still, reform school was a walk in the park compared to the county jail.

Her uncle, a supermarket produce manager, told her before she left Bartow that she was too wild and wanted to grow up before her time. Maybe he was right. Chanel didn't like to live by other people's rules.

When she decided to leave home, Chanel moved in with a white girl named Nancy. They shared a fourteen-dollar-a-night room at a cheesy motel on Nebraska Avenue. They agreed that when either of them found a john and took him back to their room, the other girl would walk slowly back to check. On this night, as agreed, Chanel was slowly scuffling her sandaled feet back to the room to check on Nancy, but she never made it home.

The killer saw Chanel walking alone, pulled up in his car, and asked her what she was doing. She walked up to the window and told him that she wasn't what he thought she was. Maybe he was in the mood for a mystery woman, an enigma. Did she mean she wasn't a hooker, or that she was a lesbian? Something different must have interested him at that moment. He talked her into getting into his car. She was young and strong, but she was no match for him physically. He was a big, six-foot-tall guy, weighing nearly two hundred pounds, who played sports regularly.

He hit her as he reclined the seat on the passenger side of his car, and he made her roll over on her stomach. He forced her to undress completely and tied her hands behind her back. He looked at her with hatred and beat her again, but he didn't have sex with her there. For the moment, he savored her suffering.

The man drove north of Hillsborough State Park to Morris Bridge Road, just south of the Pasco County line. He stopped near the entrance road to a cattle ranch. The dry dust swirled as he abruptly applied his brakes near the barbed-wire fence. He then untied her wrists and told the terrified woman to get out.

He decided to have sex with her after all and attacked her mercilessly from behind on the seat of the car. Afterward, he tried to strangle her, but she kept struggling. Strangulation is hard work; it takes at least five minutes, sometimes ten, for the clutching, frantic victim to lose consciousness. He decided to be different with a quick, execution-style bullet. Maybe she didn't even see it coming. He aimed a gun and shot her point-blank in the back of the head, then shoved her body under the wire fence.

Entering the car again, he threw her clothing out the window. Her panties caught on the barbed wire. A breeze deposited her bra atop the entrance gate, which made him smirk. He left the lacy lingerie hanging there.

A week later, a man on horseback rode up to the ranch gate. Others might have seen the bra and thought it was a joke, but from high in the saddle, the ranch hand could also see the nude corpse. He bridled the startled animal and galloped off to call HCSO.

Soon, Miller, Terry, and Dets. Cribb and Latimer arrived with Technician Peace. They discovered a figure lying facedown in the underbrush. Her body was alive with maggots that completely covered her head and genitals. Her legs stuck out from under the fence that separated the field and the road.

Her clothing was carefully collected as evidence and plastic sacks were put around her hands. After photographs were taken, her body was rolled into a white sheet and taken to the medical examiner's office. A patrol deputy remained to secure the scene, but the

rest of the team left around midnight to return the next morning.

Around one o'clock in the morning, Cribb
and Peace met at the ME's office. They took
fingerprints and X-rays, which showed some
particles from the bullet entering the skull.
Later in the day the autopsy was completed.
Police identified the victim as Chanel Williams by her fingerprints.

Back at the crime scene, detectives found a
gold post earring and a tooth. They continued
to interview employees at the K-Bar Ranch,
but the investigation was difficult and unpro-
ductive. The following day, Det. Hill went to
the motel, where he met Chanel's roommate,
Nancy. She gave him a small suitcase, some
clothing, and some letters that had belonged
to Chanel. He collected the evidence. Still, no
solid leads were turning up. HCSO looked for
similarities to other recent female homicides.
There was little to connect them, other than
that they were nude, were found in rural areas, and were prostitutes or bar girls. In fact,
there were obvious differences, including the
use of the gun, the use of ropes or ligatures,
and now, race.

Seeking help in solving the mystery, HCSO
asked the FBI to develop a criminal personality profile on the Long, Simms, and Williams murders. At this point, Loudenback
was still not considered in the same group.
When the FBI lab checked the Williams

evidence for the second time, they found both types of the red carpet fibers on her clothing. A brown Caucasian pubic hair was discovered on her sweater and semen stains on her clothing contained A and H blood group substances. The fibers matched the Long and Simms fibers, but the semen did not match that found in the Simms case. It was reasoned that this could be because they both worked as prostitutes.

Sometime later, the FBI returned the requested profile of the probable killer. It was similar to the one their Criminal Investigative Analysis Subunit had prepared on the killer of Long and Simms. This helped HCSO, but finding this killer would still be tough.

Meanwhile, the local press quickly pieced together a brief history of Chanel Williams. They interviewed her relatives and friends.

"She was kind of on the wild side," said her grandmother. "She just got in with the wrong company." Chanel's mother had this to say about her daughter's death: "We all know that loved ones have to go sometime, but you never think they'll go this way."

Six

She had it all. She was beautiful, intelligent, and born to a wealthy father, but when she was introduced to drugs in junior high school, Karen Beth Dinsfriend's life began an irreversible downhill spiral. The family lived in Saint Petersburg, where she left Boca Ciega High School in 1972, during her sophomore year. Soon she became well known to police.

While working as a bank teller in 1976, Karen was charged with grand larceny and fraud for skimming money from customers. She tried to get back on track by earning a high school equivalency certificate while in jail. Two years later, however, she gave birth to a daughter at a hospital in Bryn Mawr, Pennsylvania, and court records show that the child entered court ordered foster care within a year. Karen never recovered from this loss.

"I love my baby," she wrote sadly to a Pinellas County circuit judge in November of 1978. "My heart is so heavy with grief from being without her now. Is there not a chance for me to take her and go where I can get the help I need and have my beloved baby? . . . I want to raise her and love her. If I lose her, it would not only hurt me, but how would she feel when she grew up?"

She was denied custody of the baby. Perhaps as a result, shortly afterward, Karen was heavily into drugs again. During this time she was charged four times with using forged prescriptions in order to obtain Dilaudid, a painkiller similar to morphine. She returned to prison in 1982 for fraudulently obtaining prescription drugs in Tallahassee and was released in one year.

This time, making an effort to put her pain behind her, she moved back to Saint Petersburg and got a job as a restaurant hostess. Unfortunately, she soon came in contact with some people from her past.

"They gave Karen a freebie of heroin one night," her sister recalled, "and that was it!"

Hooked again, Karen was back on the street, trying to find money for her habit. Saint Petersburg police arrested her in January of 1984 for offering to perform various sex acts for twenty to fifty dollars. She had a bottle cap of cocaine in her jacket, and needle marks scarred both arms. She now had a tattoo of a cross on her right wrist and a tattoo of a butterfly on her buttock.

Off and on for a number of years, she had been treated at Operation Parental Awareness and Responsibility (PAR) in Largo, Florida. Counselors saw her one final time in June of 1984, when, after a six-day stay, she left without permission. The court issued an arrest warrant.

"When she left, she just dropped off the face of the earth," a counselor said. "She just ceased contact with us, which is very unusual. She was very desperate in her attitude. I think she understood the seriousness of the life-style she was involved in."

Just as her life had been a violent, nightmarish existence, so was the dreadful manner in which she died. Again, Terry and Miller were bewildered and repulsed by the bloody death scene that they were called to on October 14 in northeastern Hillsborough County. The partially nude woman lay on her left side, trussed up like an animal. Her head had been pounded, and blood flowed from her nose and ears. Her yellow sweatshirt had been pulled up close to her neck, which had been bound with rope before she'd been strangled. Her wrists and legs had also been bound with rope. Her belly was bloody and bruised, indicating that she'd been dragged there, and her entire body was bruised and dirty.

"You had to have been there," said Terry, "to smell the body and see a tortured person who had been jerked by the neck rope while she was being raped and strangled." An indelible memory of it was etched on the minds of Dets. Latimer, Osgood, Bacon, and Marsicano. Only a crazed monster of a man could have done this.

The killer had picked Karen up as she'd walked down a street near Nebraska late at night. She'd offered to have sex with him for forty-seven dollars, the, exact amount she needed for a fix. He stripped her, bound her, and raped her in the fashion that he enjoyed, which was facedown on his reclined front car seat. Then he drove to a heavily wooded orange grove, where he raped her again. As he was strangling her, he heard dogs barking nearby. He waited a moment, peering into the darkness before he got out of the car, and groped for a beach blanket that he had in his trunk. Finding it, he wrapped it around the body, which he stuffed in the trunk.

Next, he drove to another grove, got the body, and dragged it over to a tree. Here the bizarre ritual continued. She was still wearing the yellow short-sleeved sweatshirt, but the bottom of the shirt had been pulled up to her armpits, exposing her back and breasts. He covered her feet with the rust-colored blanket and lashed it in place with strips from a blue sweatsuit. He used a red bandanna to bind her wrists together in front. A long, heavy shoelace, which also tied her wrists, was lashed around her neck as well. Another shoelace was tied around her ankles for good measure. When he was finished arranging her, he threw her clothes out of his car and backed down the road.

Dr. Miller, the medical examiner, verified at the scene that the bloody ligature marks around Karen's neck had probably been made while she was still alive. Although the investigating team had recognized the twenty-eight-year-old prostitute immediately, fingerprints now confirmed her identity.

The most significant discovery was the red fibers on the victim's clothes. The binding of the victim had also become the killer's "signature," and detectives strongly suspected that this death was related to the unsolved Long, Simms, and Williams cases.

HCSO went into a more intense round-the-clock investigation as every available homicide detective was assigned to these murders. Property detectives were handling other, unrelated homicides, assaults, and suicides. Six tactical detectives were given night surveillance duty in north Tampa, where Long, Simms, Williams, and Dinsfriend had operated. This area included Nebraska Avenue and West Kennedy Boulevard. The detectives were well aware of the FBI profile and used it and the physical evidence to narrow their search for this crazed serial killer.

Seven

The public was near panic about the growing string of related murders as a modern-day Jack the Ripper stalked Tampa Bay. Extensive media coverage was given to backgrounds of victims, murder locations, photographs, and family interviews. Newspaper sales soared. Special attention was focused on the Strip, and prostitutes working there talked about their friends who'd become victims. They feared that the unknown killer could be someone they knew. The media blitzed every angle. Only the fiber information was kept confidential.

It seemed as though the city had become obsessed with the serial killer. Police teams were continually conducting interviews with area prostitutes and bar owners, and the paperwork mounted. License numbers of vehicles frequently seen in the area were recorded. This information and anything else related to the murders was put into a special computer reserved for this investigation.

Evidence from the Dinsfriend death site was flown directly to the FBI laboratory. Mike Malone confirmed a relationship to the other homicides. Sitting in his small room for hours studying the microscopic evidence, he found both types of red nylon carpet fibers as in the other cases. He also found semen and brown Caucasian pubic hairs, and a sweatshirt disclosed type A and H blood group substances. This had also been found in the Williams case one week earlier.

Malone took a break from the lenses and carefully maneuvered his six-foot frame through the partitions of the adjoining cubicles to retrieve his jacket from the free-standing coatrack. He liked to work in his shirtsleeves, but when he left the building he was always properly attired, FBI-style, in a dark suit.

Back at HCSO, Capt. Terry had rolled up his sleeves hours ago, working and waiting. The phone soon rang with still another homicide report.

On Halloween Day, 1984, Paul M. Both, 71, was operating a backhoe, clearing a ditch, when he got the scare of his life. The ditch ran parallel to U.S. 301 at the north edge of Hillsborough County, about 200 feet below the Pasco County line. A row of trees separated the ditch from the highway, and when Both stopped his backhoe, he gasped at the terrible sight of a mummified figure. As he approached, he realized to his horror that this was no Halloween prank, but the remains of a dead young woman. Adding to the eerie picture was hair still attached to her skull.

At first there was absolutely no clue as to her identity. Sheriff's deputies combed the area both on foot and by helicopter. The mummified figure had been found lying on its back, the arms and legs apart, revealing a large, empty pelvic cavity. Examination of the soil yielded no more than a plastic bandage, which was bagged.

All that was known was that the victim was white, was about five feet tall, and weighed 110 pounds. She had shoulder-length reddish-brown hair, was probably in her early twenties, and had probably been dead at least two weeks. There were no clothes, ropes, or further evidence; it was not much to go on.

Such sparse evidence made Maj. John Cacciatore reluctant to link her with the other four sex-related killings of young women that had occurred over the past five months. Still, he was leaving no stone unturned.

"The fact that the victim was not bound does not necessarily rule out the possibility that she was killed by the same person who killed the other four women," he said in a statement.

The police were stymied when the autopsy report revealed nothing new. They added more small details on her description, such as her having crooked teeth and pierced ears. An urgent appeal was made to the public, but no one came forward.

It was not until later, when the killer was apprehended, that her identity and the details of her death became known through his confession of the crime. Her name was Kimberly Kyle Hopps, known on the street as "Sugar." He had picked her up on Nebraska by a bridge at Sulphur Springs. She was a pretty strawberry blonde with smooth, long legs, and she wore white shorts. He pulled over to the side of the road; she came up and asked if he wanted a date. When asked the price, she said thirty dollars.

He took her behind an old abandoned theater by the bridge at Sulphur Springs. Supposedly they were looking for a parking spot, but when he did stop, he proceeded in his normal routine. He took her clothes off, tied her facedown on the reclined seat, and had sex with her from behind. This time he strangled her using a black collar that she wore around her neck. He then threw her body in a ditch and scattered her clothes elsewhere as he drove home.

Eight

All available law enforcement personnel were assigned to major streets and highways as tension mounted on both sides of the law over failure to catch the Tampa Bay killer. Hookers along the Strip were paralyzed with fear, hesitant to work. Police were frustrated, overwhelmed, and working too hard.

Finally, the killer made a big mistake. About 2:30 A.M. on the morning of November 3, seventeen-year-old Lisa McVey was riding her bicycle home from work down Waters Avenue. Just as she turned south on Rome, happily humming a tune, a male driving a maroon car came cruising down Waters from the opposite direction. He slowly turned the car around and passed her on Rome, studying the attractive lone rider in his rearview mirror. She had shoulder-length dark auburn hair that fell in ringlets. She was trim and athletic. He liked her looks. He crossed Sligh and, looking back again, noticed an empty van parked on the west side of Rome. Maneuvering his car into a dark church parking lot on the east side, he crossed Rome on foot and hid in front of the van. When Lisa pedaled by, he jumped out and grabbed her by the hair, pulling her off the bike.

She screamed as he pressed a gun to her throat. "I'll kill you if you don't be quiet!" he warned. She believed him and did as ordered. He forced her to walk backward across the street to his car, where he pushed her in through the driver's door. Once inside, he demanded that she remove her clothes and he felt her firm body.

My God! she thought, *Is this really happening to me? He'll kill me if I struggle.* "Do anything you want," she pleaded. "Just spare my life!"

"Nice breasts," he said. He unzipped his pants and forced her to perform oral sex on him. Afterward he warned her to keep her eyes closed and he started the car and drove off, making her continue. As he was driving along, he stopped her before he ejaculated. He pushed her back in the reclined passenger seat, touching her body, and said, "You and I are going to have a real good time, aren't we?"

"Okay," she replied tentatively. Her brown eyes widened when she got a glimpse of a gun on the seat by his right leg. Fondling the gun, he ordered her to keep her eyes shut.

After slowly cruising more residential

streets, he decided to take her to his apartment on Fowler Avenue. When he arrived there, he put a blindfold on her and helped her don her shirt and pants, but he left her underwear, shoes, and socks in the car. They walked up two flights of red carpeted stairs which had a railing on each side. Lisa would be kept hostage in this apartment for twenty-six hours.

The frightening man guided her into the bathroom and made her take her clothes off. In this room, he made her bend over and tried to put his penis into her rectum. She cried and said it hurt, and he did not go any further. They continued on into the bedroom. With her blindfold still on her, he made her lie on the floor on her back. In this position, he had vaginal sex with her and ejaculated. Afterward he told her to stand up and face the wall. He went to the bathroom, then returned for her to take a shower with him. Her hair got wet and after the shower he turned the hair dryer on and brushed her hair until it was dry.

"You have very pretty hair," he said, walking her into the bedroom. "Come over here and lie down."

As they lay down on his waterbed, he turned off the light and removed her blindfold. It was too dark for her to see him, but he touched her with cold steel and said, "That's just to let you know I still have my gun." Lisa shivered when she heard him put the weapon on the shelf over the bed.

Lisa's legs were tied loosely with a cloth strip, which felt to her like the same fabric as the blindfold. The cloth was looped around her ankles and each ankle was tied, but he had allowed ample space between her legs. She was not tied to the bed, and sometime early in the morning he untied her legs altogether and said, "I trust you now."

They stayed in bed the rest of the night and most of the next day. He touched her body and made her touch him. He had her rub his back and right arm, which he said was sore from lifting something heavy at work. He also made her say things to him about what she wanted him to do to her. He made her say, "Lick my body, lick my tits, fuck me."

He called her "Babe" a lot, since he had never asked her name. She gave him false information about where she worked and lived, and if he knew better, it didn't seem to matter. They had sex many more times and he made her perform oral sex several times. Once he had her get on her knees and stomach and he had anal intercourse with her. Afterward he said, "Thank you!"

She thought he might have drifted off to sleep on several occasions because his breathing seemed heavy, but she was afraid to do anything. Realizing that he might not really be asleep, but could just be testing her, she could not sleep herself. She lay quietly next to her captor, determined to remember every detail. Lisa silently vowed to survive in any way she could.

When daylight came, she could not see clearly through the heavy dark curtains in the room. She did see a digital clock on the headboard. He put the blindfold back on her, but they still remained in bed.

Several times he said, "I don't know why I did this. You're such a nice girl. Revenge, I guess. I just broke up with my girl and got tired of women walking all over me."

She was very frightened, although he did not violently threaten her. She did not want to anger him because of the gun, so she did whatever he asked. She specifically did not ask him to take her home. He was relaxed and even joked, "Maybe I'll just keep you." During the time that she did not have the blindfold on, he told her to keep her eyes shut and she always obeyed.

The entire time that she was there, he let her use the bathroom only twice. Once was about eight hours after she'd arrived, and the other time was just before they left. He would always follow her in. While he was using the bathroom, he made her stand near him with her eyes shut. She knew that the light was on, but even as they took another shower together, she kept her eyes shut.

While in his apartment, McVey told him that she lived with her sick father, who'd had twenty-two heart attacks. She did not tell him that her father was a double amputee, because she was afraid he would come to her house and cause problems.

He asked what she would do if he came to the restaurant and she recognized him. She managed to grin. Her large white teeth gave her a pleasant, appealing smile. As he touched her body, he said, "You're strong for a girl. You have great leg muscles." He repeated many times, "I don't want to hurt you, Babe."

He had tremendous mood swings. One minute he would be very nice, and the next minute he would be mean. When mean, he would handle her roughly and his voice would become harsh and gruff. He did not brag about having done this to anyone else.

Later in the evening, they got up. He gave her his shorts to wear, which fit her well, and a black pullover top. He blindfolded her, tied her feet loosely together, as before, and tied her wrists together, allowing sufficient space between them for movement. He also put a gag in her mouth. She did not hear him tear the strips of cloth, so she surmised that they had been prepared beforehand.

He took her to the living room, sat her on the couch, and turned the television on. One of her favorite programs, *Airwolf*, was on. Suddenly, a special news alert broke into the program with a report of a local girl's kidnapping.

"You don't need to hear that," he snapped, as he clicked the television off.

That's because I'm here, I'm living it, she thought to herself.

He asked her if she was hungry and then she could hear him in the kitchen, making sandwiches. The sandwiches were ham and bread with sesame seeds on the bread. He left the blindfold on while they were eating, and although her hands were tied, she had enough movement capability to be able to eat the sandwich and drink a soda. She wondered if the food was poisoned.

Lisa started to cry and he asked her what was wrong. She said, "Nothing."

"Bullshit. Tell me what's wrong," he demanded. She told him that she was tired of being tied up, and he said, "I don't like to see you cry, but I don't want to hurt you." He then took her back to bed, untied her, and allowed her to get in bed with her clothes on. He had on only bikini underwear. Before he took her blindfold off, he turned the light off. He kept telling her that she was a nice girl and he wished they could have met some other way.

As they lay in bed, he licked her ear and kissed and nibbled on her neck. He then took her shirt off and sucked on her breasts. He told her, "Just rest, now." He did not have sex with her anymore.

Lisa did not remember if they slept or just lay there in the dark. When the alarm went off around 2:30 A.M., he announced, "Time to get you out of here, now. Time to get up and get going." He told her again to keep her eyes closed as he helped her get dressed by putting her pants back on. When he picked up her shirt, he remarked that it was too dirty to wear, so he dressed her again in the black pullover.

Blindfolded, she went back downstairs with him to his car, which she entered from the passenger side. When she clumsily hit her head, he stopped and said, "I'm sorry, Babe. I should have guided you in." Once in the car, he put her socks and shoes back on and joked, "Isn't that service?"

McVey recalled that just before they left the apartment, before going downstairs, she heard him click the revolver and then she heard something rattle in a drawer. She thought he might have unloaded the gun, but she wasn't sure. All she could think of was how to get out of this alive.

After they were in the car, he kissed her before driving off. She was now sitting in the reclined passenger seat, dressed and blindfolded. As they left, he said he had to get gas and asked, "Can I trust you not to run?" He still had the gun with him and she had to assume it was loaded. He needed money before they got gas, so they drove about five or ten minutes to a bank. He got out of the car and she heard the sounds of the automatic teller machine buttons. Peeking from under the blindfold, she saw a white building with lights in the windows up high. He then drove to the gas station, which seemed right around the corner, and got out and pumped the gas. She never heard him talk to anyone and thought perhaps he had not paid. After they left the gas station, it seemed about ten minutes to the interstate. As they were getting on the interstate, she got a glimpse of a Howard Johnson's sign and a Quality Inn to pinpoint the location.

Lisa's mind raced as she tried to figure out a way to escape. In sideways glances, he looked pensive; maybe he was wondering if he should let her go. He asked her what she was going to say about all this. He suggested, "Just tell them some guy abducted you at gunpoint and borrowed you for a few hours."

He turned around and stopped in the parking lot at the corner of Rome and Hillsborough. He told her that he didn't want to let her go and that he might just

keep her. He hugged her and kissed her and
said that he hoped that her father got better.
He told her to stand there for a few minutes
with the blindfold on after he left. He gathered up her belongings, including her shirt,
which he had carried downstairs, and her
underwear, and told her, "Here's all your
stuff." With a casual "Take care," he left her
standing in the parking lot.

Am I going to be killed? she wondered. As
the moments passed, she knew she had sur-
vived. She fell to her knees and wept uncon-
trollably for a while before managing to walk
home. Then she called the police.

In her initial statement, McVey recalled
that when she first got into the car with her
abductor, he told her that not only did he
have a gun, he had a knife as well, but she
never saw or felt a knife. McVey also recalled
that when he first had her in the car, he
told her that he had been following her for
about a mile, from Florida Avenue. She remembered that while she was riding her bike
on Waters Avenue, she heard a car honk
somewhere near North Boulevard.

Lisa got home sometime around 4:30 A.M.
She had to knock on her father's bedroom
window to wake him, and by the time she
finally got inside, she was hysterical and cry-

ing. She even passed out. It took her about two hours to calm down.

When she stopped to think, Lisa remembered that while she was at the apartment, she promised herself that if she got out alive, she would tell the police whatever was necessary to catch this man. She never hesitated about calling the Tampa police.

Lisa described her abductor as a white male, possibly in his mid-thirties or older, because he'd told her that he was old enough to be her father. His voice, not familiar to her, was deep. While they were in bed, he allowed her to touch his face. She remembered from the glimpse she'd had of him that his hair was brown and it felt like it was about an inch long in a layered cut. He had thin eyebrows and a short mustache. His face felt rough, as if he hadn't shaved in a couple of days. It seemed like he had a big nose and small ears, and his teeth seemed good. His lips seemed skinny and his eyes seemed small. She estimated that he was considerably taller than she and that he was compact, with a slightly overweight build. He was not overly muscular, although he'd seemed strong at first, when he'd grabbed her. His legs and lower back were hairy, but he did not have hair on his chest. He did not wear glasses, did not smoke, and did not drink or use drugs while he was with her. He also did not wear jewelry. He was wear-

ing jeans, possibly a white shirt with red
trim on the shoulders, and sneakers. When
he dropped her off, he was wearing some
kind of baseball-type cap because when he
hugged her, she felt the back of the cap. He
did not have any noticeable foreign accent.
She described the gun as a revolver, silver
or chrome-colored with a brown grip, possibly four inches long.

She described the car as dark red or maroon in color, two-door, full-sized vehicle.
The dashboard and steering wheel were red.
The seats and interior walls were white. On
the dashboard was a brown strip with the
word "Magnum" in silver letters. There was
also a digital clock with green numerals on
the dashboard. The white seats were divided
by an armrest. She did not remember the
carpet but thought there were floor mats,
maybe black. She caught a glimpse of the
back seat when she first got into the car and
it seemed empty. The vehicle had an automatic transmission, a radio tuned to a local
station, and electric door locks that did not
have a knob at the top. The car also had
either a mechanical engine noise or a noisy
muffler, and it seemed to vibrate a lot.

Her temporary prison, his apartment, was
light-colored stucco on the outside. She recalled that he'd had to open some kind of
gate before they'd got to the stairs. The door
and the interior walls were white. The car-

peting was red. Upon entering, she thought there was a bedroom to the left and a bathroom to the right, then the living room and kitchen. The bathroom was pink, and a picture of an owl was on one wall. There was a rug around the toilet and a pair of dirty jogging-type shoes or sneakers on the bathroom floor. These were white with a medium blue stripe on both sides, laced up, with a little chicken or rooster emblem on the sides. The bedroom also had red carpet and a waterbed on which there was a lightweight bedspread. Weights were on the bedroom floor, a silver bar with gray weights. There was also a fan on the floor.

In the living room there were a couch and a coffee table and possibly a chair near the kitchen. The television was to the left of the couch, the kitchen to the right. Lisa was able to see the light of the television. The couch was finished in a flat velvetlike fabric. She did not actually see the coffee table but heard him set things on it. While she was in the apartment she could hear noises from the outside: cars, television, and voices.

With Lisa McVey's vivid recall of her capture, her abductor's apprehension was more certain.

The HCSO urged the Tampa Police Department to send their rape case evidence to the FBI fiber specialist, Mike Malone. If this abduction and rape could be tied to the serial murders, it would be a definite break-through toward solving the homicides. HCSO felt the McVey case could be related to the murders because of some similarities, and at least now they had another law enforcement agency looking for the same man. Questions which could not be answered, however, were: Why did he allow Lisa to go? Did he fall in love with her? Did he actually want to be caught and stop killing, or did he simply feel omnipotent and never expect to be caught?

Nine

On November 6, 1984, a third law enforcement agency became involved in the unsolved case of the Tampa Bay serial killer when the remains of another young woman was found in neighboring Pasco County. Decomposed human body parts were discovered by thirty-five-year-old Linda Phethean on her ranch near Zephyrhills as she was horseback riding with a student. They were trotting down Brumwell Road, a heavily traveled dirt road, when they decided to take a shortcut across the field. A repulsive odor hit their nostrils as they came upon body parts that had been severed and scattered through the field. Hurriedly leaving that sickening sight, they galloped off to call the sheriff. They had returned when the patrol car of deputy sheriff Chris White roared up the dusty road and stopped. Both women wanted to talk at once.

"There are human body parts all over that field," the student gasped, her small body shaking, "and it's hideous!"

"I ride horseback on this road every day," said Linda, maintaining a businesslike composure. "My riding students use it and my husband jogs on it regularly. I can't understand why someone hasn't found this before."

"Just a minute, ladies," Dep. White said calmly, gesturing toward his vehicle. "I want you to go over and sit in the car and wait for me."

He started toward the field but abruptly turned his considerable girth around. "First I need to know if you disturbed anything."

They shook their heads. "We just took a quick look and got out of there as fast as we could!"

White could buy that. He nodded and walked slowly into the grassy field. The odor of death was overpowering. Drawing closer, he came upon a skull and upper torso clad in a ribbed knit tank top. A heavy shoelace and a piece of fabric were twisted around the neck. He leaned over and almost gagged. A heart-shaped pendant necklace was still around her neck, and dark body fluids stained the ground under the decomposed torso. He'd seen enough.

"Hand me the radio phone," he said to the women back at the car. When he got Dispatch, he made his report and asked for immediate help.

The Pasco County Sheriff's Office and

the Florida Department of Law Enforcement responded in large numbers. Members of each team promptly went about their routine tasks. Long-haired and mustachioed, Sgt. Ken Hagin talked to the two women extensively. Barbara Bohlken, a no-nonsense FDLE officer who wore no makeup, put up a perimeter crime scene barrier and grids so that anything located could be recorded. On the grid they logged the position of part of a skull, a scalp of blonde hair, a leg bone, a foot bone, panties, a knit tank top stained by postmortem fluid, ligatures, a heart-shaped necklace, and an earring. Each item was marked by a flag on a stick, logged, and photographed. Dets. Curtis Page and Bill Ferguson of PCSO and Laura Rossiau, FDLE, continued to lead a human chain through the field.

As it was collected, chief medical examiner Dr. Joan Woods carefully examined the evidence. She estimated that the victim had been dead for perhaps two weeks and that the body had been in that field for the majority of the time. She requested that all recovered remains be delivered to her office.

At her lab in Largo, Sgt. Ken Hagin watched Dr. Woods as she continued the examination and autopsy. Since she could find no previously existing bone injuries on the young female, Dr. Woods deduced that her bones had been gnawed by animals. The victim had died a violent death. A nine-inch cord, fashioned like a leash, had been tied twice around her neck, finishing in a double knot. A piece of cloth was also around her neck, and a heavy shoelace had been used to bind her wrists. She had probably been strangled to death, since there was no evidence of bullets.

Dr. Woods called in Dr. Kenneth Martin, a dentist, for his assistance. He could not detect any injuries to the jaw or teeth. Dr. Woods also coordinated with anthropologist Dr. Curtis Winkler. He determined that the bones were from a Caucasian female, about twenty years old and five feet, five inches tall.

Due to the similarities to the Hillsborough cases, the Pasco County sheriff contacted HCSO and sent their evidence to the FBI lab in Washington. Three central Florida law enforcement agencies were now cooperating on a growing series of seemingly related sexual murders. Although Lisa McVey had provided new leads, the list of victims was unknown and growing at an alarming rate.

All Florida newspapers carried news reports and pictures of the skeletal remains of the Pasco County victim on November 7 and 8. These articles noted similarities to the previous homicides of six young women found in Hillsborough County. Detectives had characterized four murders as sexually

motivated crimes, probably committed by the
same person. Each woman had been killed
in a different manner: one had been shot,
one strangled, another stabbed, and the
fourth asphyxiated.

On Friday, November 9, Lt. Gary Terry,
HCSO, made a series of telephone calls to
set up a meeting for that afternoon in the
Ybor City office of HCSO. The rapid esca-
lation in the number of murder/rape victims during the week, including the Tampa
rape of Lisa McVey and the unidentified
Pasco County victim, called for quick and
decisive action. Now there were three law
enforcement jurisdictions involved and the
media were giving this case daily attention.

The meeting was held around 4:30 P.M. in
Maj. Cacciatore's office. Included were representatives from TPD, FDLE, HCSO, and
PCSO. They discussed any details available
on the current homicide/rape cases. Presently, fiber, hair, and semen evidence connected the cases. There was also a pattern:
all were bound, nude, or partially clothed
young females found in remote areas. An an-
nouncement was made that Hillsborough
County Sheriff Walter C. Heinrich was in
the process of establishing a joint task force
comprising the agencies present. The task
force would consist of about thirty officers
assigned fulltime. The entire resources of all
agencies would be committed as needed, in-

cluding human resources, aircraft, and vehicles.

When the one-hour meeting was over, experienced detectives like Steve Cribb and Lee Baker from HCSO and Ken Hagin from PCSO were eager to identify and stop this sick killer. They all realized that the new joint task force, starting on Monday, would require a higher level of intensity, if that was possible.

Ten

It was as though a mythical monster was trying to satisfy his lust with human sexual sacrifice, but the craving was too much to be appeased. Now a tortured woman was found dead each week in a configuration more grotesque than the one before.

On Monday, November 12, a sign painter, Drake Reed, was sent to repair a sign on the Orient Road overpass near Adama Drive in Tampa. He parked his truck near the base of the sign, climbed up on the platform, and went to work. The base of the structure was located on a forty-foot-wide, steep dirt incline that formed the approach to the Orient Road overpass. Behind this sign was a small woods. After working for half an hour, Drake took a break and looked at the local area from his high perch. *Good location,* he thought. Businesses to the north side of the overpass were open twenty-four hours, and a heavy industrial area with daytime traffic lay to the south.

He really liked his job, but today he felt

a restless expectation. As he was looking around, something in the grass down the incline caught his attention. He seemed drawn to it. He hurried down the platform and slid and tumbled himself halfway down the incline with underbrush tearing at his jeans.

Then he saw her, about four feet away, a sight that would remain with him in nightmares. The badly beaten young woman's face was a bloody mass. Part of her nose was missing, either as a result of the beating, or from her having been pushed along facedown. Around her neck were the now-familiar noose and rein. Rope burns on her body suggested that she had been bound in preparation for being raped. Her legs had been forced open in an unnaturally wide spread. Among her clothing, which had been strewn near her, was a flowered top that had been ripped off her body. This top had fecal matter on it. Nearby blue jeans did not have this matter on them, which indicated that the feces had come from repeated sexual assault after she had been forced to disrobe. When the Tampa police were called and Sgts. Sluga and Price responded, they also called in HCSO because of the similarity of this case to their other recent homicides. Det. Howard Smith, TPD, had the area around the body cleared of heavy vegetation to provide better working space. The hands of the victim were

covered with paper bags and sealed to pre-
serve any evidence.

Lee Baker turned to Det. Cribb with a low
whistle and a smile. There on the jeans were
small particles of reddish carpet lint. The
FBI would have this soon, and if it was what
Baker thought, it would tie this homicide to
the others. The fiber was carefully placed in
a glass vial. There were also a short piece
of fuzzy white string and some brown hairs
that could be the killer's, since the girl was
blond.

The tired and lined face of Baker bright-
ened again. Inside the pockets of the jeans
he found a driver's license issued to Kim
Marie Swann. Steve Cribb ran his fingers
through his thick dark hair and grinned. It
was his lucky day, too. They'd found a nap-
kin with a name and phone number on it
and two traffic citations from Hillsborough
County that could be checked out. The pa-
pers were wet but readable.

Due to the complex nature of the crime site,
Det. Smith decided to take a TPD helicopter
up to see if an aerial view would reveal anything else. Afterward he joined Fletcher,
Cribb, and Baker at the medical examiner's
office, where Dr. Lee Miller was examining
the body.

The victim's battered face was extremely
discolored and puffy. There were ligature
marks on both wrists and arms above the el-

bows. Rope marks were around her neck, and she had definitely been strangled. Dr. Miller estimated that she'd been dead for two or three days.

Cribb and Fletcher were assigned to drive a truck to the FBI in Washington with the evidence.

Later, when Fletcher returned to the TPD detective division with Det. Smith, they learned that HCSO had dispatched a deputy to the home of Kim Swann's parents. They called to ask the deputy to bring the parents and other relatives in for interviews.

Talking to the parents, the detectives learned that Kim had moved back home about a month before with her child. She had lost her job and was forced to give up her apartment. Her parents had last seen their daughter on Friday afternoon, when they'd passed her car, driving near their home. When they arrived home there was a note from Kim saying that she planned to visit the bank and would eat dinner out, but would be home early. Since she often stayed overnight with friends, they weren't concerned when she did not return Friday night.

On Monday, they called HCSO and reported her disappearance. The exhausted parents continued the lengthy interview. They stated that Kim often visited certain local bars, including Michael's near Ne-

braska, O. C.'s Lounge on Fowler, and P. J.
Liquors. They said that she had used nar-
cotics in the past, but recently they'd noticed
a change in her personality. She'd become
moody and had lost weight. They admitted
that she did drink occasionally, both out and
at home. What she was wearing when she
disappeared was not known, her mother said,
because Kim often traded clothes with
friends and with her two sisters.

Sandra Snyder, the victim's sister, confirmed her parents' account of Kim's habits.
When asked if her sister would be willing to
go with a stranger to a bar or allow herself
to be picked up off the street, Sandra stated
that this would probably happen. Sandra related that Kim had worked at the Sly Fox
Lounge and one night had met three men
there. They'd gone to a party where all three
men had raped her and she'd ended up in
the hospital. This incident was not in police
files.

A computer check of Kim's car revealed
that it had been impounded on Monday
morning by request from La Petite Academy, a private nursery school on Humphrey
Street, just west of Dale Mabry. At Homicide, Det. Gassi had the vehicle transferred
to the impound lot and processed as evidence.

The Swann investigation continued the
next day, when Det. Smith visited Kim's

mother and sister at their Carrolwood home. They checked Kim's closet and decided that one pair of blue jeans, a dark blue sleeveless top, and a pair of blue canvas wedge-heeled shoes with straps were missing. When Smith examined the room and found some photographs, there were ten people in the pictures that the family did not know.

"You know those other girls who were murdered here recently," added her mother nonchalantly. "Kim told me she knew two of them."

Smith was startled. There were just too many similarities here: the Tampa Strip association, young nude girls with rope marks, murdered and left in open areas. There was no doubt in Smith's mind that Kim Swann was the serial killer's latest victim.

Eleven

The following press release was issued on November 14, 1984:

JOINT INVESTIGATIVE
TASK FORCE
ON AREA MURDERS
FORMALIZED

Hillsborough County Sheriff Walter C. Heinrich, Pasco County Sheriff Jim Gillum, Tampa Police Chief Robert Smith, with Danny Johnson, Florida Department of Law Enforcement, and Dick Ross, Federal Bureau of Investigation, today formalized a joint investigative task force into the recent murders of young women in Hillsborough and Pasco Counties. Although area law enforcement agencies have been coordinating their investigative efforts on these murders since their inception, the participating agencies feel colocating investigators in the same facility and designating an investigative supervisor and

*media coordinator would best serve the in-
vestigations.*

*The investigative team will operate from
the Hillsborough County Sheriff's Office, located in the Ybor City section of Tampa.*

*Lt. Gary Terry, Detective Division,
Hillsborough County Sheriff's Office, has
been designated as the team supervisor, and
Sgt. Carl Hawkins will serve as the media
coordinator. Sgt. Hawkins can be reached by
calling the Sheriff's Office.*

*The special investigative team will exam-
ine the circumstances surrounding the recent
murders to determine connections, if any,
among them, and to gather information and
evidence that may lead to the apprehension
of the person(s) committing these crimes.*

On November 14, 1984, the initial task
force meeting was scheduled at HCSO, Ybor
City, in classroom A, a windowless room opposite the elevators on the second floor.
There were ten folding tables with chairs.
Near the front of the room were a black-
board and a lectern. All assembled were
homicide or sex crime detectives experienced
in this type of investigation. Dets. Smith,
Fletcher, and Price arrived from TPD. Dets.
Ken Hagin and Tom Muck represented the
Pasco County Sheriff's Office. They were
greeted by Terry, Cribb, and Baker from

HCSO and were introduced to others from FDLE and the FBI.

Law enforcement meetings seem predictable. Attendees usually arrive ten or fifteen minutes early, go to the room, find the coffee, and shoot the breeze. This meeting was no exception, and by nine o'clock, people were ready for business.

Everyone was briefed on the nature of the task force and the need for protecting the confidential information connecting the locations. The victim locations and numbers made HCSO the logical task force head and Ybor City the central operating location. The task force commander established procedures which formed teams composed of detectives from different agencies. This blending of responsibilities ensured that all agencies were equally involved in all aspects of the investigation.

All of this was conducted in a matter-of-fact manner, but as the meeting was ending, word came that caused tremendous excitement. It was from the Micro Analysis Unit of the FBI in Washington. The Lisa McVey evidence contained the same fibers as those found on the other serial homicides. Greatly expanded information was now available to the task force about the murder suspect, including descriptions of his car, his apartment, and his bank. Immediately the task force was ordered to reassemble across town at the TPD Detective Division for an emergency briefing.

Det. Polly Goethe, TPD, gave the group a detailed description of the suspect, obtained through her McVey investigation.

After the briefing, task force members were instructed to go to the University Square Mall parking lot at 6 P.M. to meet Lt. Terry, Sgt. Latimer of HCSO, and Sgt. Price of TPD. When they arrived, the task force members were divided into teams. They were given areas in the northeast section of Tampa to search for the vehicle and residence. When a team completed its area search, it would report in to search coordinators at 46th Street and Fletcher to get a new assigned area. This routine but vital search turned up no car or apartment all night.

The pace of task force activity intensified on November 15. In the morning, Dets. Cribb and Staunleo of HCSO and Dets. Saladino and Goethe of TPD served subpoenas at several banks for automatic teller machine records covering transactions between 2:30 and 4:30 A.M. on November 4. These subpoenas were drawn and executed based on the McVey statement that her kidnapper had used an automatic teller machine. All banks that had had transactions during that period provided the data requested. Dep. Harrell of the HCSO Aviation

Division flew to Tallahassee and picked up a printout of Dodge Magnum vehicles in Hillsborough County. The printout had been requested from the State Department of Motor Vehicles for all vehicle identification numbers starting with the code number for Dodge Magnums. He arrived back at the task force office just after lunch with the fifteen-page printout.

The task force teams were still actively searching for the apartment and automobile. Dets. Apsey (HCSO) and Smith (TPD) visited possible apartment complexes such as the Oaks Condominium to see if the floor-plans matched Lisa's detailed description. Realtors and apartment managers were all helpful and suggested possible locations. All of these were checked without a match.

Finally, a big payoff came when two detectives with the motor vehicle printout on their front seat got their first good scent of the suspect. Dets. Wolf and Helms, sipping coffee, were on cruise patrol down Nebraska Avenue when through the maze of fairly slowly moving oncoming traffic they spotted a red Dodge Magnum like the one Lisa McVey had described. They knew the drill.

They flashed the car over and got out to check the man's license. Date of birth: 10/14/53; address: East Fowler Street,

Tampa; name: Robert Joe Long. *Bingo.*
They smiled and walked back to their car
as if to check something. Actually, they
needed a moment to savor their good for-
tune. They had been thoroughly briefed,
but more time was needed to compile evidence against Long. Should he be found,
he was to be told that police were looking
for a robbery suspect, which would explain
why he'd been pulled over.

Long, certain he finally had been caught,
became very cooperative. He agreed to be
photographed and waited anxiously while
the field interrogation report was written.
He was dumbfounded but relieved when he
was allowed to go. He smirked at the feckless
detectives as he sped off.

Long's name appeared on page fourteen
of the computer printout of registered owners of Dodge Magnums in Hillsborough
County. Other policework determined that
he had used a Barnett Bank honor card at
the Florida National Bank automatic teller
at 58th Street and Fowler Avenue on November 4 at 3:49 A.M.

When task force members visited the Parole and Probation Office in north Tampa,
they could not view Long's file without a
subpoena, but the supervisor gave them the
information by reading it to them.

Robert Joe Long, also known as Bobby
Long, was on probation for three years for

an aggravated assault earlier in 1984 in Hillsborough. He had been arrested for rape in Dade County in 1974, but the charge had been reduced and he'd been placed on probation. His record indicated that he'd had a very difficult time getting along with his initial probation officer, a woman. When he moved to north Tampa there had been no problems.

This information was all reviewed at the task force headquarters. Based on it, the case was reviewed with Assistant State Attorney Michael Benito for probable cause and an affidavit was prepared for the arrest of Long for kidnapping and sexual battery. Also prepared on this evening of November 15 was a vehicular search warrant.

Meanwhile, Long was back in his apartment, two hours after being stopped. Surveillance teams, using aircraft to minimize the chances that Long would spot them, were being used to complement the ground units. Late in the afternoon Long left home in a red Dodge Magnum and went to the post office on 56th Street in Temple Terrace. Then he returned home, but immediately left again and drove to the laundromat at 56th and Whiteway. He then proceeded north on 56th, west to the main entrance of the campus of the University of South Florida, and north to the outdoor tennis and handball courts.

Long sat in his parked car for a while, reading a newspaper. After this he moved to a bench in the racketball area. Det. Pickard was right on the job and passed within three feet of Long. He reported that Long was wearing blue and white jogging shoes, blue jeans, and a gray T-shirt with "Samurai" printed on the back. Long had casual conversations with a dark-haired white girl and a tall, thin, white male with short blond hair. At a quarter to six, Long left the campus and returned to his apartment.

That night Long's ex-wife, Cynthia, called Bobby Joe to coordinate his visit with the children during Thanksgiving weekend. During the conversation, Long asked her if she had heard about the girls getting killed in Tampa. She replied affirmatively, and Long said, "It's really rough out there. That's why I tell you and Holly [Cynthia's roommate] to be careful."

He stayed in his rooms until about eleven on the morning of November 16, at which time he drove to his old residence on Meadowbrook Drive. This was the same address listed for Long on the computerized list of vehicles. He left there and drove back to Temple Terrace Post Office, and finally back to his apartment on Fowler. Between noon and 1:30, Long cleaned his car and discarded refuse in a nearby dumpster. Dep.

James Mosher observed this and retrieved the discarded evidence.

Long left his apartment again and headed north on 56th Street to the Gulf station at 56th and Fletcher, where he vacuumed his car. He then drove west to Dale Mabry to the Main Street Cinema, where he parked and went inside. Det. Turner also went into the cinema. The movie was a Chuck Norris action film, *Missing in Action.*

The surveillance team contacted the task force by radio and had the vacuumed materials picked up as evidence by a marked patrol car. Deps. Martinez and Angel collected the contents in a plastic evidence bag with the station attendant's permission.

Meanwhile, the task force had been very busy. The search and arrest warrants were reviewed and final copies were prepared for the judge to sign. The task force then consulted the Behavioral Science Unit at the FBI Academy for guidelines on interviewing Long. A special agent from the lab in Washington was flown to Tampa to assist in crime scene searches and for immediate comparison of fibers from the suspect's apartment and vehicle. An aircraft was standing by to carry the agent to the closest FDLE lab that had the required special microscopes.

In an afternoon meeting, the task force

was advised of the warrants and the following teams were designated:

1. An arrest and security transport team to physically arrest Long. Two of these officers were to interview Long after the arrest
2. A vehicle seizure and search team
3. A residence search team
4. A neighborhood survey team to interview Long's neighbors prior to the release of information to the media.

Suspense mounted as the task force teams assembled near the Main Street Cinema to wait for Long to come out. This was more dramatic than anything going on inside the theater. They were prepared with warrants to arrest him on the spot. While they were waiting, two officers checked the rear tires of Long's car and found the unique pair that had been identified in the murders. Team members in plain clothes were anxiously waiting inside a shopping mall store that afforded a good view of the theater and parking lot.

At four P.M., with police and media ready to pounce, Bobby Joe Long exited the theater and started to cross the parking lot toward his car. Dets. Radford and Davis ran up behind the startled suspect and arrested him. Det. Cribb advised Long that he was under arrest on the specific charges of the warrant. The group of officers escorted Long to his car and read him the search warrant for his vehicle. Det. Cribb then read Long his Miranda rights. It all took fifteen or twenty minutes. The arrest was completed only thirty-six hours after the task force had been formed. Their work, however, was just beginning.

Dets. Winsett, Price, and Smith transported Long to his apartment and read him the search warrant. In Hillsborough County, authorities prefer to serve a search warrant while the owner of the property is there to witness the search. Long was embarrassed and uneasy. There were many law enforcement vehicles and officers present. Long asked if it was necessary for him to be present and he was told that he could waive that right, which he did. About twelve officers from the task force residence search team began to gather evidence.

Long was taken to the HCSO interrogation room, where, with Dets. Winsett and Smith providing security, Latimer and Price began the interview. The FBI agent who had prepared the criminal personality profile was present and had briefed the interviewers that Long would most likely cooperate if they displayed both authority and a thorough knowledge of the case.

Long signed a consent-to-interview form

and requested a cup of coffee, which was
provided. Latimer, Price, and Long began
talking about 6 P.M.

When Bobby Joe Long was arrested in the
Main Street Shopping Mall parking lot, the
task force read him the *vehicle secure and vehicle warrant.* His 1979 Dodge Magnum was
hoisted onto a flatbed wrecker truck. Darryl
Gibson of Gibson Wrecker Service towed the
car to the HCSO evidence garage on Morgan
Street in Tampa. Det. Tom Muck rode in the
wrecker, and Dets. Cribb and Fletcher kept
the evidence car within sight from their vehicle for the entire trip.

The car was secured in the Morgan Street
garage by 6:30 P.M. Immediately a sample
of the right front floor carpet was removed
and released to special FBI agent Michael
Malone for comparison. Malone was quickly
flown to the FDLE lab in Sanford, Florida,
to use their comparison microscope to study
the fiber sample.

A short time later, Malone telephoned
HCSO confirming the fiber match between
those from Long's car and those found on
the victims. This physical evidence would be
used by the investigators interviewing Long,
together with an explanation of the significance of hair, tire, and blood comparisons,
to convince him to confess.

For four hours on Friday night and all day Saturday the vehicle was processed for evidence. Pictures were taken inside and out. The interior and exterior were checked for latent fingerprints. The interior of the car was carefully disassembled so they could check for fibers, fingerprints, blood, and other physical evidence. Task force members Cribb, Pickard, Moore, Muck, Mosher, Tillis, and Wilson all participated. Each item was carefully marked, cataloged, and packaged for examination as evidence.

Twelve

About six P.M., after Long had signed a consent-to-interview form, he settled back with a cup of coffee and started talking to Dets. Latimer and Price. He did not look very threatening now. In fact, it was hard to believe this very average man had kept an entire city in a grip of fear for six months. The seriousness of the situation finally hit Long as he sat crumpled in the chair. There was no hostility; he was just a country boy ready to tell his story.

Latimer started with the easy stuff, trying to build a comfortable relationship. Long stated that he had been divorced for five years but rarely saw his children, who were now ten and eleven, because they lived with their mother in Hollywood, Florida.

With the personal updates concluded, they got down to more serious questions, such as Long's criminal past. When he was asked about his arrest in Miami for rape in 1974, Long protested that it was a completely different situation from the crime at hand. He claimed that he was married when he'd engaged in an affair with a 16- or 17-year-old girl who consented to sex. Long was in the military and her father was an officer in the service.

Pressing on with the psychological tug-of-war, Latimer asked about Lisa McVey's kidnapping and rape. Long stated that he did not know what had motivated him to abduct Lisa. He said that he'd driven over to Dale Mabry earlier in the evening in search of a drink, then he decided against stopping at a bar and began to head home. As he drove east on Waters, he passed McVey, who was riding her bike home. Long had turned around and followed her south on Rome from Waters, passed her, and crossed Sligh. He'd seen a van on the west side of Rome, south of Sligh. Long parked in the church lot on the east side of Rome and crossed the street to hide by the van.

He lurked in front of the van, hoping fate would send Lisa his way. Lucky for him, she hadn't changed direction. As she approached, Long jumped, grabbed her by the hair and pulled her off her bicycle. He told her he had a gun and warned her not to scream. Long dragged McVey across Rome to his car. He pushed her into the vehicle through the driver's door. Once they were inside, Long ordered her to keep her eyes closed and to take off her clothes. Long would not discuss the details, but stated simply that he'd had sex with McVey. Was this vicious killer, the man who'd raped and strangled women like roped animals, finally getting a conscience? Latimer knew this would be a long night.

Long continued his story, saying that he then got scared and left the parking lot, driving down several residential streets, getting lost before finally arriving at his apartment. He had dressed Lisa inside the vehicle, blindfolded her, and walked her up the stairs to his apartment. He reluctantly admitted he'd had sex with the victim numerous times in the next twenty-four hours.

Sometime on Saturday, he fixed her a ham sandwich, took her into the living room, and put her on the couch to feed her. Long stated he tied her hands and feet so she wouldn't try to escape. Lisa told him she was cold, so he covered her with a bathrobe. They had talked about how it was too bad they'd had to meet this way. He claimed that at one point she said she did not want to leave. She told him her father had numerous heart attacks and was a very sick man. Long asked her if her family would be worried, but she acted nonchalant. He wasn't sure if this was to pacify him, or if she was sincere. Long said she was a nice kid, and he wished he hadn't attacked her.

He recalled throwing the gun off the

Courtney Campbell Causeway somewhere into the bay two days after he'd abducted Lisa. Long hoped that his desire to grab women for sex would fly out the window along with the gun. Bobby Joe sadly admitted that his desire to abduct and rape women did not leave him, but he had not committed any crimes in the last week or so, since kidnapping Lisa. He seemed proud of this fact.

Long denied being on drugs, said he rarely drank alcohol and did not suffer from memory lapses. Latimer smiled silently as he noted these declarations, which would later help refute any claims to the contrary by some wily defense attorney.

Latimer asked why he had not shot Lisa. Long replied that he had unloaded his gun and put the bullets in the trash in case he was tempted to shoot her. Some remnants of humanity had remained, after all. Long warned that no female was exempt from attack if she was out late and alone.

He admitted going into depression when he was unemployed or had a hard time at work and said he racked up highway miles to relieve tension. In the past two years alone he had driven 50,000 miles. Latimer remarked that he must really use up the tires, hoping Bobby Joe would say something to explain the unique tire marks that had been found at the scene of the murders. Long confirmed that he had used at least a dozen tires in the last two years, replacing the two front tires in May. Both rear tires had been on the vehicle for all of 1984.

Long stated he had made the blindfold used on Lisa two days before her abduction. He'd put it in his glove compartment knowing it would come in handy, although he didn't know exactly when or on whom he would use it.

Latimer set a verbal trap by flattering Bobby Joe's intelligence. Long bragged that he was a certified advanced open-water scuba diver and also an X-ray technician. Latimer was familiar with this and discussed qualifications and the schooling that Long had gone through to achieve these qualifications.

"Do you know what the term 'physical evidence' means?" Latimer inquired. "Hair, blood, fingerprints, you know, that kind of stuff. Now they even have fiber evidence and tire tread impressions."

Their eyes met and they studied each other. Finally, Long said, sure, he'd heard of physical evidence. Breaking the tension, the door opened and Sgt. Price rejoined the interview.

He asked Long if he had ever picked up any prostitutes. "Yes," he responded. "In Miami."

"Ever picked up any prostitutes in Tampa?"

asked Price. "I'd rather not answer that question," Long responded.

Latimer opened an envelope and tossed down pictures of five murder victims, one at a time. Images of Kim Swann, Karen Dinsfriend, Chanel Williams, Michelle Simms, and Lana Long spilled on the table in front of Bobby Joe.

"Ever seen them before?" he was asked. Long replied, "No," and asked to use the restroom. Latimer and Price accompanied him to the bathroom next to the interview room.

Upon his return, Long was asked if he remembered the conversation on physical evidence, and he said he did. He was then asked if he had ever heard of the quality work done by the FBI lab in Washington, DC. Long said that he had, and he was told that two expert lab technicians from Washington had been brought in to help gather and compare evidence on today's search warrants. Latimer specifically described the tire on Long's vehicle as a Vogue tire with a gold-ringed whitewall that had been turned inside on the rim. Long was told that this particular tire had shown up at two other crime scenes that had not been discussed yet.

At this point, Long observed that it sure seemed that the complexion of this interview

had changed since Sgt. Price had left the
room. Long's exact words were, "I think I
might need an attorney."

Sgt. Latimer told Long that things had not
changed and urged Long to be honest with
himself. Surely he knew when he was picked
up today that it would lead to the discussion
of these crimes.

Latimer then told Long that they had hair,
fiber, and tire evidence in the murder cases.
He said that they were not trying to build a
case on him now, since the case was already
made through evidence and witness information. Now they simply wanted his side of the
story.

Bobby Joe Long then sat back in his chair,
smiled, and said, "I guess you've got me
good."

"What do you mean?" Latimer shot back.

"Yes, I killed them," Long answered. Asked
how many, he said, "All the ones in the paper.
I did them all."

The detectives sighed, pulled up chairs,
and sat down. They asked him to start at
the beginning and to describe each case and
the victims.

He said his first victim was an Asian girl.
She never told him her name, but he found
out through the newspaper that it was Lana
Long. He picked her up as she was walking
east on Fletcher at Nebraska Avenue. He
asked her if she wanted a ride, and she re-

sponded, "Yes." She got into the car and
he asked her if she wanted to go get a
drink. She replied, "No." He then drove
her to a wooded area off 22nd Street, between Fletcher and the Way Apartments,
which are on 131st. At that point Long reclined the passenger seat and made the victim lie facedown at knife or gunpoint (he
didn't remember which). He made her take
off her clothes, tied her hands behind her,
and then drove by an unknown route to 301.
He succinctly described going south to Symmes Road, west on Symmes to East Bay
Road, and to the south deadend of East
Bay. There he drove around a barrier down
a dirt area to a fence which bordered a cow
field. Long said he had sex with the victim
in the car, but he would not elaborate on
the sex act. He took her out of the car, at
which time she began to fight him. He hit
her several times in the face with his hands
and then strangled her with something (he
didn't remember what, but it was definitely
not his hands). He left her facedown, her
hands tied behind her back, her legs pulled
far apart. He threw her clothes onto Symmes Road en route to 301 to return to his
apartment.

With amazing detail, Long recalled that
the next victim was Michelle Simms. She was
hooking on Kennedy, around Rene's Lounge.

"Okay, and how did you go about picking her up?" asked Latimer.

"Just pulled her over. She was a hooker." He smiled.

"What did you say to her?" Latimer continued.

"She asked me if I wanted a date, and I said yeah. She said fifty bucks and I said all right."

"Then what happened?" Latimer prompted.

Long sighed and replied, "She got in the car. I don't know if she had a room or not, but I didn't want to go there." He drove her to some buildings on Dale Mabry, where he made her undress, tied her up, and drove her to the Lithia-Pinecrest area, where he had sex with her. He drove to some back roads to where she was found.

"Okay, and what happened then?" Latimer asked.

"I tried to strangle her with something, not with my hands, with something else, but it didn't work. And then I stabbed her with the knife."

"Okay, you tried to strangle her and she wouldn't choke out and then you stabbed her with a knife?"

"Well, first I hit her in the head with something, a club kind of thing."

"Why did you hit her with a club?" Latimer asked.

"I didn't want her to suffer."

"So you were trying to knock her out so that she wouldn't suffer while you were doing what?"

"Killing her. I can't believe I'm saying this stuff."

"You need to talk about it for yourself. You tried to strangle her the second time and you said she wouldn't go out, so what did you do then?" Latimer tried to get back on track.

"I took her out of the car and stabbed her with the knife."

Long said he then threw her in the bushes on her back, threw her clothes out next to her, left her tied up, and took back roads to get home. Although he threw the knife in the woods next to his apartment after this murder, he later retrieved it on November 15.

Next he described the killing of Elizabeth Loudenback. She was walking on Nebraska Avenue, north of Fletcher. Long asked her if she wanted a ride. She said yes and got into the car. As soon as she got in he pulled over, stopped the car, tied her up, and took her pants off. Then he drove her to an orange grove in Brandon. At this time he had sex with her in the car, untied her, and allowed her to put her clothes on. Long was going to let her go free, but his exact words were, "She jerked me around." He strangled her with a rope and also took her purse, which he later threw out of the car somewhere in Tampa. However, inside the purse was a bank card and a piece of paper with a four-digit number on it. He had cards of his own and knew how to use them, so within a few hours he had used hers. He had trouble at one place on Dale Mabry but used the card two times at the Florida National by his apartment on East Fowler and again on Dale Mabry. Eventually, he said, he threw the card away.

Long said his next victim was Chanel Williams, a black girl. He saw her walking down Hillsborough Avenue, at about 15th Street, and asked her if she wanted a ride. She replied, "I'm not what you think I am." They talked for a while and she got into his car. He pulled a gun on her, tied her up, and took her clothes off. Long then drove her to a dirt road on Morris Bridge Road, which came up to a gate. There he had sex with her in the car. Long tried to strangle her, but she would not strangle. He took Williams out of the car, walked her around front between the gate and his car, and shot her one time in the back of the head. He then dragged her to some bushes, threw her clothes out, and left. He stated that the gun he used was the same gun used on Lisa McVey and on Mary Hicks in 1984. [When arrested, Long was on probation for aggravated battery in connection with this attempted kidnapping of Hicks.]

Swallowing some water, he began talking about Karen Dinsfriend. She was walking on Hillsborough Avenue about one or two in the morning. He asked if she wanted a ride and she offered to have sex with him for forty-seven dollars. She told him that was the amount she needed for a fix. He agreed, and she got into the car. He bound her with a rope and took her clothes off before proceeding to an orange grove about a mile away. He had sex with her in the car and then took her out of the car and strangled her.

At this point Long stated that he heard dogs barking and they sounded very close, so he wrapped her body in a blanket and put her into the trunk of the vehicle to drive to another dirt road about a mile away. Long went down this road, stopped, removed the body, and dragged her behind a tree into the first row next to the road. He left her hands and feet tied and left her clothing at the scene.

Continuing to recite details of the murders as if it were a game, Long spoke about the decomposed body on 301 at the county line. He said the victim told him her name was Sugar. She was walking on Nebraska by the river in Sulphur Springs. He recalled that this murder occurred after Chanel but before Karen, but he did not remember the day or date. He related that he pulled over. The victim approached his car and asked if he wanted a "date." He asked, "How much?" She answered, "Thirty dollars." She got into the car and they drove behind the old theater. Long tied her up, took her clothes off, and drove out 301 by the county line. He pulled off the road to a clearing where he had sex with her in the car and strangled her with a black collar that she wore around her neck. He remembered leaving her tied up and throwing her down an embankment into a ditch where she landed face up. He randomly tossed her clothes out the window on his way back to Tampa.

The next case he discussed was the girl whose bones had been found on Morris Bridge Road in Pasco County. Long said he had picked her up after Dinsfriend on Nebraska by the Malibu Grand Prix, which is in the area of Skipper Road. Long asked her if she wanted a ride and she said, "Sure." Once inside the car, she asked Long if he wanted a date. They drove to a dirt road off Skipper Road, behind Cheek's Lounge. He tied her up and stripped her, then drove her to where she was found off Morris Bridge Road in Pasco County. Long said he had sex with her in the car and then strangled her.

He dragged the body off the road, left her panties there, and left her tied up with shoelaces.

Sgt. Price asked if Long knew about Vicky Elliott, a missing girl who had been en route to work the midnight shift at the Ramada Inn at Busch and Nebraska and never arrived. Long said he saw her walking on Nebraska and asked her if she wanted a ride. She said yes and got into the car. Long pulled down a side street and had started to tie her up when the girl pulled a pair of scissors out of her purse and stabbed him in the chest. The wound was minor, but it angered him. They fought, but he finally got her tied up and took her to the deadend off Old Morris Bridge Road. There they had sex in the car. He strangled her and took her body and clothes elsewhere. At this time Long drew a map marking an "X" at the location where he'd put the body. At the end of the interview, Latimer supplied this information to Lt. Terry so they could dispatch a unit to try to locate this victim.

The next victim Long talked about was Kim Swann. He said she'd been weaving down Dale Mabry by Whisperlake Apartments when he'd pulled up next to her and asked her to pull over. He asked her if she wanted to get a drink and she agreed and got into his car. After she entered the car, she apparently sensed something was wrong

and started to fight him. He said in order
to control her and calm her down he'd
struck her numerous times in the head and
face with his fist. After she was subdued, he
took her clothes off and drove her to a road
which runs off Skipper by Cheek's Lounge.
Here she began to fight again. This time he
tied her up and strangled her. He drove her
to an overpass off Adamo Drive and dumped
her body over the guard rail about midway
up the overpass on the east side. Long estimated it happened about two or three A.M.,
two days before she was found. Long stated
that he did not know the name of the road
but was sure that it went north off Adamo
Drive and that the overpass was just as you
turned off Adamo. He stated that he was
northbound when he'd stopped and dumped
the body. When first asked what he had
done with Swann's clothes, Long said he had
thrown them out somewhere after leaving
the body. Then he corrected himself, saying
that he had in fact thrown her blue jeans
and top close to the body. He remembered
that she was wearing black leather boots. He
further stated that due to the victim's intoxication and all the trouble she'd given him,
he hadn't had sex with her. Long also related that Swann had had diarrhea in his car
and he'd used her clothing to clean up the
car prior to throwing it out next to the body.
Upon concluding the conversation regard-

ing Kim Swann, Latimer and Price attempted to gain more detailed information concerning specific dates of each murder. Long couldn't give the dates, but he could relate the order in which he'd committed the murders. He also said that when he removed his victim's clothing he threw them on the floor of his car. He stated that he did not keep any articles belonging to the women except the bank card taken from Elizabeth Loudenback.

Long was questioned with regard to what kind of preparation he'd made prior to each murder and how, in fact, he'd picked his victims. He said the only preparation in most cases was buying rope in twenty- or thirty-foot lengths at places like K-Mart. As for the victims, he stated they were picked totally at random.

After discussing all of the homicide cases, Long was asked if there were any other crimes he might have committed that he would like to talk about. Latimer asked him to go back a little to 1982, when he was in California. Long said he was there from March to September of that year. Latimer asked if there were any other murders that he had failed to mention. Finally he asked Long if he'd ever been to Washington state. Long answered "No!" and added, "I'm not that Green River guy!"

Latimer asked about a rape and robbery

which had occurred in New Port Richey, where a woman was home alone. He said the suspect had come to her home inquiring about the house, which had a For Sale sign in the yard. Long admitted to this offense and further related that he had used the same gun, the Ruger black steel gun with gold around the trigger, in other crimes. He recalled that he had gone to the front door and told the victim he was interested in the house. The woman had asked, "What do you want to know?" At this point Long pulled his gun and forced the victim inside. He took her into a bedroom and raped her. Before leaving, he stole some jewelry, mostly rings and chains, which he pawned under his own name in Tampa.

Latimer asked him if there had been other rapes. Bobby Joe admitted that there had been others in Florida. When asked if he wanted to talk about them, Long replied, "Not particularly. I don't particularly want to talk about any of this."

"Well, Bobby," said Price, "what he's obviously saying is that we might as well get it all while we're at it."

Latimer added, "Bobby, the victims are still going through the fear that whoever raped them is still out there and it gives them peace of mind for the rest of their life to realize that you're not still out there, that they're not susceptible, and that maybe they can relax and start a normal life again. So anything you can do, do it to help the victim. Get it off your chest."

"Here's a good example," offered Price. "When you let McVey out of the car and she contacted me, I really didn't believe the situation. I said, 'For God's sake, why in the world didn't you stop the first car you saw on the street?' She said to me, 'I was scared to look at another car!' See, she didn't know who would be in the next car."

Long said that he could understand that and continued to talk about rapes he had committed. He said that down in south Florida, while he was still married, he would pick his rape victims from the classified ads in the newspaper. He remembered about fifteen where he answered each ad, went to the house, and once inside, raped them.

Long complained that he was tired now, but Price couldn't help asking him, "When did you feel we were getting close to you?"

"When those guys pulled me over a couple of days ago," answered Long.

"Are you working anywhere now?" Latimer asked casually. Long smiled. "No, but I have some good prospects!" He paused before observing, "That was a joke."

"I'm tired, too," admitted Latimer.

Just before the interview ended at 9:45, Long got a cold drink and said, "You guys know that the only reason you caught me is because I let Lisa go." Then he asked Sgt. Price to tell McVey that he was really sorry for what he had done and added, "You know, letting Lisa go makes it worth getting caught for killing all the others."

Thirteen

When the taped interview with Price and Latimer was finished, Long asked if he could call his ex-wife, Cindy, in Hollywood, Florida. Permission was granted, and a poignant conversation which lasted about thirty minutes ensued.

"Remember what we talked about last night?" Bobby Joe asked.

"You mean the girls?" she replied.

"Yes," he said softly.

"Well, what about them?"

"I did it." There was silence still as death. Finally she sobbed, "You're joking."

"I wish I were," his voice broke, "but I'm not."

Cindy asked him if it was something she had done while they were married, or if she was the cause of it. He assured her that whatever had made him murder had happened long before their relationship. Sgt. Latimer came on the phone and confirmed that Long had been arrested for murder.

"Please tell the kids," Long pleaded to his

ex-wife, "that I've been killed in a car wreck."

Later, in a statement to the police, Cindy said that Long was basically a good person who loved his children very much. Even after the divorce, he remained a good father who would help her with the children when needed. She said that when he came to visit her he was always very nice and she enjoyed having him around.

The reason for the divorce was that they argued a lot, mostly over finances. She said he didn't hold a job very long and often their money would run low, causing a heavy burden on the family.

Concerning their sex life, she said that while they were married, it had been good. He had never tied her up during sex, and she did not consider him to be oversexed or kinky in any way. She remembered that he took some nude photographs of her when they were first married, but she didn't consider that to be anything particularly unusual. He never asked to take photographs of them engaged in any sexual activity.

She had no idea why her ex-husband had committed these murders and could provide no information whatsoever about any other crimes he might have committed. She seemed completely shocked that her ex-husband had become a serial killer.

The additional murder of missing Vicky Marie Elliott that had not been known until Long had confessed to it during his interview, when he'd marked the location of the body on a map. Det. Latimer delivered the map to Gary Terry. Dets. Winsett and Novak were sent to investigate.

They arrived at the north deadend of Morris Bridge Road, about half a mile north of Fletcher Avenue, around 10:15 P.M. on November 16. There a dirt road led to a barbed-wire fence. Beyond that was a small patch of high grass with small trees on the west side of the I-75 bypass.

Both officers searched the small overgrown area adjacent to the wire fence. Soon Novak discovered Elliott's skeletal remains, exactly where Long had indicated he'd left her. The detectives called for backup and a patrol unit guarded the scene until the next day.

The next morning when the two detectives returned to the scene, they were joined by Maj. Cacciatore, Det. Docbo, and Technician McGill. McGill took photographs of the wooded area and the remains. The skeleton was lying on its back with its right arm extended outward, the left arm closer to the side. The legs were straight. The skull was on its right side with some reddish hair surrounding it. No clothing, jewelry, or identification were nearby. A black-handled pair of scissors, eight or nine inches long, lay in what would have been the victim's vagina, with the sharp ends pointed toward the abdomen. Extensive rusting of the blades indicated that the scissors had been in the body cavity prior to decomposition.

Long had confessed to strangulation in this case, and McGill found the hyoid bone in three separate pieces. Closer examination revealed that the victim's upper and lower teeth had fallen from their sockets. The bones were bagged separately by body parts and sent to the medical examiner's office.

An intensive search about seventy feet from the victim revealed more evidence. The detailed report submitted by Maj. Cacciatore listed envelopes containing a brown leather shoe with shoestring; a white cloth handkerchief; a brown/yellow nylon stocking; a brown leather shoe without shoestring; a yellow cloth with knot; two pieces of brown cloth; a pink plastic tampon applicator and white tampon; the partially rusted scissors; and an envelope containing all known cranial hair of the victim's. These were forwarded to the FBI lab in Washington, DC, and it was requested that this be examined for hair, fibers, blood, and semen and compared with other Long sample evidence from his person, car, and apartment.

Twenty-four bags of dirt and vegetation

were removed from under the skeletal remains and identified by body location. Technicians double-sifted each bag separately and recovered four additional items: one incisor tooth, one bicuspid tooth, two small human bones, and one painted toenail. Dr. Vickie Lindauer, DDS, made a positive identification from Elliott's dental records.

Investigation revealed that Vicky Elliott had been a petite, pretty twenty-one-year-old redhead with a personality that matched her bright hair. She had worked at the Ramada Inn coffee shop on the corner of Busch and Nebraska. She chose to work the eleven P.M. to seven A.M. shift, since it paid forty cents more an hour and the tips were better.

Usually she walked the mile from her apartment to the coffee shop by following the railroad tracks. She became alarmed when men yelled at her from cars and she began carrying scissors in her pocket for protection. On the night of September 7, Elliott had asked a neighbor for a ride to work, but when the friend had gone to pick her up, she'd already departed. She never arrived at work.

Her manager, Mickey Newburger, said, "We knew something was wrong instantly. Vicky was never late. Always so punctual." She had given her employer two weeks' notice, saying that she wanted to return home to Muskegon, Michigan, to become a paramedic. "She had already bought her plane ticket back to Michigan before she disappeared," Newburger said. "It was still lying on her bed when we opened her apartment."

It was not until Long's confession on November 16 that Vicky's friends or mother knew she was dead. Lora Elliott suspected that her daughter was probably in terrible trouble, but she wasn't prepared for this news.

"I wasn't relieved," she said, although her daughter had been missing for two months. "I had myself hoping that she would still be found alive."

In their November 18 Sunday editions, local newspapers carried photographs of the recovery of Vicky Elliott's remains as the ninth victim linked to Long. Her obituary was overshadowed by the front-page stories of Bobby Joe Long's dramatic arrest.

The *Tampa Tribune* headline was, "Fibers Tie Suspect To Killings." The stories recalled ". . . the six-month reign of lustful and lethal attacks on young women in the Tampa Bay area." There were many pictures of Long, as well as profiles and photos of his victims, plus maps showing where the dead girls had been found.

Since most of the victims worked or lived near the Nebraska Avenue Strip (several had been dancers; three had had arrest records for prostitution), lively interviews with other working women were numerous. The bumps and grinds came to a temporary halt as these women reacted in nervous relief to the news of the arrest of a man accused of brutally murdering nine young women.

"It actually made me cry," one dancer said. "It's like I can leave work and not worry about getting killed!"

Some said they would always be apprehensive, looking over their shoulders for another threat like Long, but none said that it would stop them from working.

"The money that we make at night goes to our kids during the day," explained one twenty-one-year-old dancer and mother of a baby daughter.

At one point, police had passed around a photo of Long, and this brought a colorful response from Dennie Valdez, manager of the Starlite Lounge.

"These places are real zoos," he admitted. "The guy lived in the neighborhood. Of course he's been in here. One cop told me to call whenever someone 'unusual' walked in. If I called every time someone unusual-looking came in," he smiled, "I'd be on the phone right now."

A prostitute recounted the grim side of her profession. "Every car you get in could be some freak that wants to kill you or severely hurt you." She still considers it big money and is willing to take the risks. It's just a job to her.

Sly Fox owner Lamar Golden said, "I'm glad it turned out he's not a street person," speaking of the suspect Long. "Street people don't kill each other. The majority of them are pretty vulnerable and not that hard to be friends with."

Fourteen

The task force officers had no reason to expect their rapid success in bringing in Long. His capture, however, produced a new avalanche of leads, evidence, and most of all, associated paperwork.

The team that searched Bobby Joe's apartment gathered a large volume of evidence for analysis. Pictures were taken and furniture and bedding were thoroughly vacuumed for victims' hair. There were many trash bags full of miscellaneous property belonging to Long. Two suitcases were seized that contained financial records and telephone address books, plus photo albums and loose pictures. At least twenty-five unidentified white females appeared in these photographs. Most of the photos were lewd, with some showing explicit sex acts. Apartment dumpsters and grounds were searched, and Long's knife was found in his apartment.

On the Friday night when it was gathered, this material was all placed in the evidence room for future study. It was cataloged and

sent to the FBI for analysis. Team members
wrote reports and processed evidence in the
Long surveillance, arrest, and confession.
They did the same for the Swann and Elliott
cases.

Almost all of the task force detectives took
a day off on Sunday, November 18, after
working around the clock for a week in the
investigation and arrest. Bobby Joe Long,
however, had a memorable day.

At nine A.M., Long was taken from his iso-
lation cell in the Hillsborough County jail
on Morgan Street to the tiny, windowless
court room in the building. The six-feet-tall,
one-hundred-eighty-pound Long swayed
from side to side as he walked shackled and
handcuffed. He was dressed in a blue
jumpsuit stenciled with the jail's insignia. He
stopped about two feet in front of the bench
where County Judge Perry Little was presid-
ing.

Long was in court less than three minutes.
When Judge Little asked him if he had spoken with an attorney, he responded,
"Right!" Long stood silently between two
detectives, sometimes looking at the judge,
other times glancing down at the handcuffs
on his wrists. Judge Little charged Long
with eight counts of sexual battery and nine
counts of kidnapping. The extra kidnapping
charge was for the Pasco County victim abducted in Tampa. The final charge was for

violation of his aggravated assault probation. The judge refused to allow bail for the murder charges. Judge Little advised Long of his legal rights and he was returned to his cell.

On Monday, November 19, the investigation continued at full speed. Long had called the unidentified victim, who had been found in the ditch on U.S. 301, by her street name, "Sugar." He identified the contact location as Nebraska Avenue by the river in Sulphur Springs. This name and location directed local detectives to prostitute Kimberly Kyle Hopps, a twenty-two-year-old white female, who had been last seen by her boyfriend.

Her friend, Donald Jones, had filed a missing persons report on October 7, 1984, stating that his fiancée, Kimberly Hopps, had disappeared. When detectives interviewed him, Jones said that the last time he had seen her was at the corner of Nebraska and Hanlon, near the Orange Motel. They were arguing about money.

Sometime around 8:30 P.M. on October 4, Hopps got into what he thought to be a maroon 1977 or 1978 Chrysler Cordova. It was being driven by a white male, and from pictures in the newspaper, Jones knew the driver was Bobby Joe Long. He said that the car headed west down Hanlon and out of his view. The last time he saw Kimberly she was wearing pink shorts, a light pink blouse with string straps, and a black scarf.

Jones identified both Long and the photograph of Long's vehicle, stating that what he originally thought was a Chrysler was, in fact, the Dodge Magnum. Dets. Muck, Pasco, and Rick Duran of Tampa picked up Kimberly's photos, records, and prints from HCSO. Her prints were compared with the body found in the ditch, and her identification was confirmed.

Dets. Hagin and Muck learned of a missing person report that might possibly fit the description of the Pasco County unidentified victim. A Virginia Lee Johnson, AKA "Ginnie," had been missing since mid-October. Sharon Martinez of Tampa had filed the report, and when Hagin called her, she described Virginia as an eighteen-year-old white female who had straight blonde hair and was about five and a half feet tall. Martinez also told Hagin that Johnson had been living somewhere on Orange Avenue with a man named Alvin.

Hagin arranged to meet Martinez at about seven P.M. While he and Muck were talking with her, Alvin drove up. He introduced himself as Alvin Duggan, age thirty-nine, and said he lived on Orange Avenue. He was a thin man with narrow shoulders, a scruffy hairline, and long sideburns. He said that he had periodically allowed Johnson to stay at his house, and he voluntarily took the group to his residence to show the detectives Johnson's personal belongings there.

Looking for possible clues, the detectives found ninety dollars in cash and a slip of paper giving Johnson's date of birth as February 23, 1966 and her mother's name as Sonja Peters of Danbury, Connecticut. Martinez said that Virginia had severe alcohol-related problems and was skin-popping heroin and cocaine. She worked as a prostitute to support herself.

The detectives asked Duggan and Martinez about the floating-heart pendant, which was on the skeletal remains found November 6 in southern Pasco County. Martinez said that a necklace and pendant fitting that description had been given to Virginia by Robert Seebeck. Det. Muck called Seebeck, who acknowledged the necklace gift and referred them to his daughter, Michelle, who also knew of the necklace and pendant.

Ken Hagin then telephoned Robert Peters, Virginia's stepfather, who said that he had not seen her for three or four months but believed she was living in the Tampa area. He also offered information that Virginia had seen Dr. John Gish, a dentist, sometime in the spring of 1984. Hagin called Dr. Gish in Danbury and he confirmed the visit. He said the dental chart was in his office and to call there the next day. In doing so, Hagin verbally compared the dental chart completed by Dr. Ken Martin in Pasco County to the one of Dr. Gish. Gish agreed to send the dental X-rays by Express Mail to Martin so he could confirm the identification. When the X-rays arrived on November 21, Hagin hand-carried them to Dr. Martin in Holiday, Florida. He positively matched the postmortem dental X-rays to those taken by Dr. Gish. Hagin then notified the task force at HCSO and the Danbury police, who notified Johnson's family.

This identification was, however, too late to be included in the task force press release of November 21, 1994. This release stated:

Hillsborough County Sheriff Walter C. Heinrich, Pasco County Sheriff Jim Gillum, Tampa Police Chief Robert Smith, along with Danny Johnson, S.A.C., Florida Department of Law Enforcement, Robert Butler, S.A.C., Tampa Office of the Federal Bureau of Investigation, and Hillsborough County State Attorney E. J. Salcines announced on November 16, 1984, the arrest of Robert J. Long, charging him with eight counts of murder, sexual battery, and kidnapping. One additional murder charge is pending in Pasco County.

The arrest of Robert J. Long came after a joint investigative task force was formed on November 14, 1984, to probe various related murders of young women found in the area.

Robert J. Long, 31 years old, has been charged with the following crimes:

1. Murder, Sexual Battery, Kidnapping. Victim: Ngeun Thi Long, 22 years old. Found May 13, 1984, deadend of East Bay Road, south of Symmes Road, Riverview. Cause of Death: Strangulation.

2. Murder, Sexual Battery, Kidnapping. Victim: Michelle Denise Simms, 22 years old. Found: May 27, 1984, Park Road north of I-4, Plant City. Cause of Death: Stabbing with signs of strangulation.

3. Murder, Sexual Battery, Kidnapping. Victim: Elizabeth B. Loudenback, 22 years old. Found June 24, 1984, southwest corner of Turkey Creek Road and Whitehead Road, Turkey Creek. Cause of Death: Pending.

4. Murder, Sexual Battery, Kidnapping. Victim: Chanel Devon Williams, 18 years old. Found October 7, 1984, Morris Bridge Road, 1/2 mile south of the Pasco County line, Thonotosassa. Cause of Death: Single gunshot wound.

5. Murder, Sexual Battery, Kidnapping. Victim: Karen Beth Dinsfriend, 18 years old. Found: October 14, 1984, Fort King Highway, 4 miles north of Florence Road, Thonotosassa. Cause of Death: Strangulation.

6. Murder, Sexual Battery, Kidnapping. Victim: Kimberly Kyle Hopps, 22 years old. Found: October 31, 1984, east side of U.S. 301, 225 feet south of Pasco County line, Thonotosassa. Cause of Death: Pending.

7. Murder (Pending). Victim found November 6, 1984, Morris Bridge Road, 2.2 miles north of Hillsborough County line, Pasco. Cause of Death: Pending.

8. Murder, Kidnapping. Victim: Kim Marie Swann. Found November 12, 1984, east of North Orient Road and north of East Adamo Drive, Tampa. Cause of Death: Strangulation.

9. Murder, Sexual Battery, Kidnapping. Victim: Vicky M. Elliott. Found: November 16, 1984, north deadend of Morris Bridge Road, west of Interstate 75, north of Fletcher Avenue, Tampa. Cause of Death: Pending.

10. Sexual Battery, Kidnapping. Victim: Juvenile.

The Joint Investigative Task Force will continue to gather information and evidence,

Bobby Joe Long, 34, an unemployed X-ray technician living in Tampa, Florida, before his arrest.

Ngeun Thi Long, 19, also known as Lana Long, danced in clubs on Tampa's infamous "Strip." She was Long's first known victim.

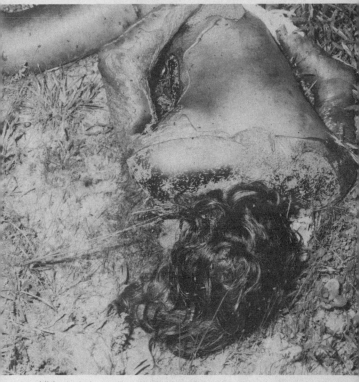

Hideously bound and slaughtered, Ngeun Thi Long's maggot-infested body was found near Hillsborough Bay, displayed in what would become known as Bobby Joe's signature position.

Long's second victim, Michelle Denise Simms, 22. A former beauty contestant, she died a drug-addicted prostitute.

Quiet and trusting, Elizabeth Loudenback, 22, was friendly with Long and became his third victim.

Loudenback's jean-clad body was found in
an orange grove.

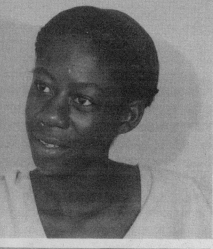

The fourth victim, Chanel Devon Williams, 18, was shot to death by Long and dumped in a field.

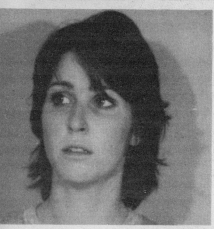

Karen Beth Dinsfriend, 28, supported her drug addiction through prostitution. Imprisoned twice, she was released from prison in June, 1983, and became Long's fifth victim.

Police found Dinsfriend with her legs and wrists bound with white cords. Long strangled her to death with the same kind of cord.

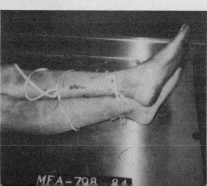

MFA-798 84

Prostitute Kimberly Kyle Hopps, 22, went by the street name "Sugar." She was Long's sixth victim.

Authorities theorized that Long choked Hopps to death using her own black cloth collar.

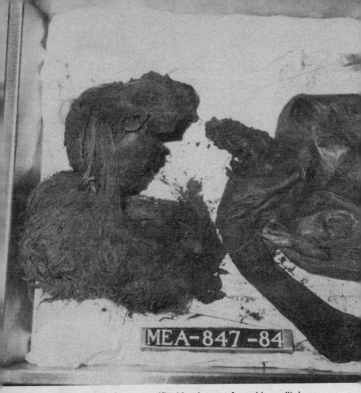

MEA-847-84

When Hopps's mummified body was found in a ditch on
October 31, 1984, some of her hair was still attached
to her skull.

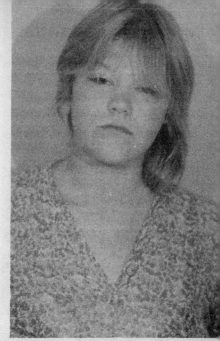

Victim seven, Virginia Lee Johnson, 18, was born in Danbury, Connecticut, and worked the Tampa "Strip."

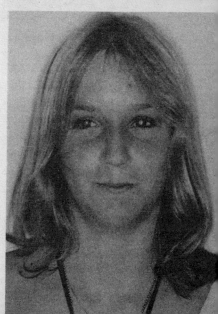

Kim Marie Swann, 21, Long's eighth victim, was found raped and strangled on November 12, 1984.

Victim nine, Vicky Marie Elliot, 21, was a waitress at the local Ramada Inn and often walked to work along the railroad tracks carrying a pair of scissors for protection.

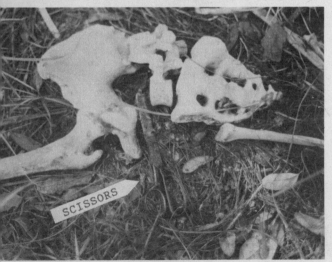

SCISSORS

When police found Elliot's skeletal remains, the position of the scissors found among them indicated that the killer had jabbed them into her pelvic area.

Lisa McVey, 17, was abducted by Bobby Joe on November 3, 1984, as she was riding her bicycle home from work. He held her hostage for 26 hours, raped her repeatedly, and finally released her. She later identified Long in court.

McVey's bicycle as it was left after her abduction.

The Hillsborough County Sheriff's Office illustrated the locations of Long's victims to help with the complicated investigation.

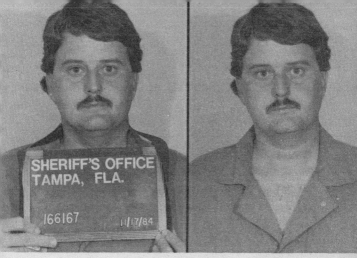

Bobby Joe upon his arrest for murder.

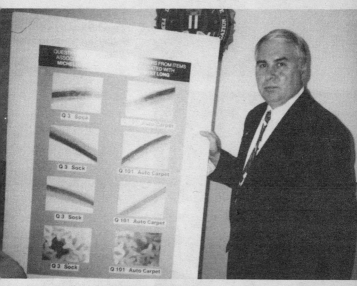

Special Agent Michael P. Malone, Hairs and Fibers Unit
Laboratory Division of the FBI, displays a chart showing fiber
evidence that linked Long to the death of Michelle Simms.

Major Gary Terry, Hillsborough County Sheriff's Office, headed the successful task force that caught Long.

Detective Lee Baker played a key role in the Bobby Joe Long murder case.

Michael Benito represented the State's Attorney General and prosecuted Bobby Joe. Benito is now in private practice.

Bobby Joe Long at his first hearing.

Eight years later, Bobby Joe enters a Volusia County
courthouse to learn his death sentence was upheld for the
murder of Simms.

The commemorative display of the Bobby Joe Long case at the
Hillsborough County Sheriff's Office.

and cooperate with other jurisdictions who seek to determine connections, if any, between Robert J. Long and alleged crime victims within their area.

Fifteen

The six months of news stories featuring the murders was followed by numerous detailed accounts of Bobby Joe Long's capture, confession, and murder charges. Inevitably, officials tried to link other victims and unsolved crimes in this time frame to Long.

On November 19, the body of a nude white woman between the ages of sixteen and twenty was found floating in the Hillsborough River. She had been strangled with some type of device. The victim had shoulder-length brown hair and brown eyes, was five feet, one inch tall, and weighed about ninety-three pounds. She had a red-and-yellow butterfly and two iris flowers tattooed on her left breast.

HCSO contacted newspapers and television requesting the public's help in identifying the girl. The cold water had made it difficult to determine time of death. The woman was never identified due to lack of evidence, but she certainly fit Long's victim profile.

Likewise, two other cases were submitted

to the FBI. On September 4, 1984, a white girl was found dead in the woods near a golf course east of Tampa. Plaster casts of tire impressions were made of auto tracks at the scene. Her clothes and hair samples were sent to the FBI for comparison and analysis after Long's capture. They, however, found no evidence linking this case to Long.

On November 22, the skeletal remains of a female with her hands bound was found in rural southern Hillsborough County. The remains were estimated to be at least six months old. The victim was identified as Artis Wick, reported missing March 28, 1984. Although this is the tenth homicide attributed to Long by the FBI and HCSO, he was never formally charged in this death and did not include it in his initial confessions.

Long's classified ad rape confession caused a flurry of newspaper articles, telephone calls, and task force activity. The day after the newspaper accounts of his general confession, it was reported that Long fit the description of the man who had raped and robbed a twenty-year-old woman in her home north of Port Richey on March 6. In this case, the woman reported that a dark-haired man, about thirty, knocked on the door at her Ranch Road home. He asked the price of her home, which was for sale. After a brief conversation, he produced a .38-caliber revolver, pointed it at her head, and forced her inside. He blindfolded her, tied her to a chair with clothesline, forced her to undress, and raped her. He then fled, taking some jewelry and her wallet. This victim, who had moved out of state, would not return to file charges. Silver-topped salt-and-pepper shakers and jewelry from this robbery were later found in Long's apartment.

Pinellas County prosecutors formally charged Bobby Joe Long in the May 29 rape and robbery of a Palm Harbor woman. This crime occurred two weeks after the Lana Long murder. The victim placed an advertisement in the newspaper to sell some bedroom furniture. She was called by a man who asked directions to her residence. When the man arrived, she took him to the room in which the furniture was located. The man pulled a knife and threatened to kill her. Then he bound, gagged, and sexually assaulted her, hitting her several times in the face. He left her on the bed, bound and gagged, and took two rings from her fingers, a heart pendant she was wearing, and other items from her jewelry box. He also stole a cable television converter box, which the task force later found in Long's apartment.

The task force prepared photograph kits containing pictures of Bobby Joe Long and other young men. These were sent to reported rape victims for possible identification of their attacker. Six victims in Florida failed to identify Long's picture.

The Marion County sheriff listed Long as the suspect in a December 1983 rape and a November 1983 murder. St. Lucie County notified the task force that they were considering Long as a suspect in rape cases in 1974, 1978, and 1983. Clearwater police contacted the task force with rape cases from March 1981 and August 1983 that fit Long's style and description.

Estimates on the number of women raped by Bobby Joe Long vary from as few as 25 to over 150. In his confession, he stated that the rapes began in 1974 and lasted for 10 years.

When arrested, Long was on probation for aggravated battery in connection with attempted abduction at gunpoint on April 5, 1984. He forced Mary Hicks into her Jaguar in the Carrollwood Shopping Center lot, demanding that she drive him away, but she escaped by wrecking the car. The judge fined Long $1,500 for damages to the car and withheld judgment on aggravated battery but placed him on three years' probation. His arrest violated this probation, and this case was included in his Hillsborough County charges.

* * *

There was a strange twist in the Long investigations that was caused by coincidences. Long had begun a commercial diving course at the College of Oceaneering in Wilmington, California, in January of 1982. He completed the course in September of 1982 and returned to West Virginia to work. He lived with his parents.

In the summer of 1982, the bodies of five prostitutes from the Seattle-Tacoma Strip were found murdered in the Green River in King County, Washington. A task force was formed to find this serial killer. It was unsuccessful, and the task force was disbanded. From late 1982 through early 1984, more skeletalized bodies were discovered again in the woods by hunters. A total of twenty-seven bodies were found, but not the killer. The police wondered if he'd left the area, as Ted Bundy had, to continue to murder in a new location.

Long left West Virginia and returned to Florida in late 1983. The serial murders of young women left in remote areas began in the Tampa area in May 1984. Florida officials wondered if Bobby Joe Long could be related to all of these murders. The dates seemed to fit. On November 15, prior to Long's identification or capture, Tampa area newspapers wrote headline stories comparing the Seattle killings to the Hillsborough County-area killings. The possibility of a connection was discussed by high-level Hillsborough detectives from May 1984 on, and even after Long's capture and confession, the Tampa task force continued to investigate any possible link.

The task force checked out Long's activities while he was in California in 1982. Det. Lee Baker, HCSO, contacted Det. David Reichart of the Green River task force, Seattle, Washington. They interviewed a classmate from Long's diving class about Long's activities in California. The transcript of this interview with Brad McCormick of Vancouver, British Columbia, was extensive. Nothing in the interview suggested any criminal activity by Long. During part of the course, Long had shared an apartment with McCormick, who had first-hand knowledge of Long's school and home activities.

During his confession to nine murders and many rapes, Long specifically denied being connected to the Green River murders. In a thorough check of his activities during this period, no incriminating evidence was found.

The task force investigations lasted through early December. Many hours were spent writing reports, clearing missing persons reports, and processing evidence. Evidence in each case had to be identified, cataloged, sent to the FBI, then received back and filed.

On November 27, Dets. Cribb and Fletcher drove an entire vanload of evidence from Tampa to the FBI lab in Washington. It included Long's sofa, much of the interior of the car, packages of vacuumed particles, the car's tires, packages of soil from murder scenes, Long's diving equipment, and the rope used to bind victims. This all arrived in Washington on November 28.

They returned to HCSO from Washington December 1 with a load of evidence the FBI had already processed. It was placed in their evidence room.

Task force members from law enforcement agencies other than HCSO returned to their regular duties on December 4, 1984. A small group continued operations. Their work as a unit is used as an example of what can be accomplished when law enforcement agencies cooperate.

Sixteen

Kenova, West Virginia, where Bobby Joe Long was born, is in the far western part of the state where Kentucky, Ohio, and West Virginia meet. The town of about 5000 is separated from neighboring Catlettsburg, Kentucky, by the Big Sandy River. It is seven miles west of Huntington, West Virginia, on the Ohio River, and sits where the rivers meet.

Modern chamber-of-commerce writers would call Kenova a "multimodal transportation center." The locals would laugh at that sophisticated description. They would tell you endless stories about the continuous barge traffic on the murky Ohio River. There are railroad tracks slicing the town from every direction. Kenova is a rail hub where the Norfolk & Western, the Chesapeake & Ohio, and the Baltimore & Ohio Railways meet. It is situated between the coal- and the steelmills and between the grain belt and populous East Coast.

Kenova is made up of conservative country

people who left the farm and moved into town. They came seeking steady jobs and a better life in the factories and rail yards.

It was in this uneventful little town that Bobby Joe's parents, Joe and Louella, met and married. Louella was just seventeen, a very pretty girl with a good figure and flirtatious smile, when she met Joe. He was twenty-three and had rugged good looks. His wild behavior attracted her immediately. In a fever of love, they were married in 1952. In a year a son was born. Soon love cooled during months of constant arguing. They were separated, and in 1955, divorced.

Louella was determined to get away from the dull smoke and cinders of trains and factories. She dreamed of the good life in sunny Miami until it became an obsession. One day she desperately grabbed her two-year-old son and boarded a bus headed for Florida. She was destined to be disappointed again. Florida was not the romantic land of plenty she'd seen in the movies.

When she and her young son arrived in Miami, she took whatever jobs she could find. While others cared for Bobby Joe, she hustled at low wages as a barmaid, waitress, and carhop at a drive-in restaurant. Her son was cared for by the families who owned the rooms Louella rented, and she felt guilty about leaving him while she worked.

"He had a very tormented childhood," his

mother admitted. "Some of the places we lived weren't good. I was scared to death, but I didn't know what else to do."

During the daytime Louella and Bobby Joe were inseparable. She would play with him at the beach or take him to children's tourist attractions, where she spent money she could not afford. Still, after these days together, he would cry each night when she left.

"He was such a sad little boy back then," his mother recalled.

Frustrated and searching for a more stable life, Louella began making short, intermittent visits back to West Virginia. She started seeing her ex-husband once again, and in the fall of 1960, she decided to remarry him. Louella and her son, however, still continued to live in Florida for long periods of time. Bobby Joe entered the first grade in Florida, but before the school year ended, they were back in Kenova. He finished the school year at Kenova Elementary School, but although he was bright and alert, he was not promoted to second grade.

The next year, seven-year-old Bobby Joe repeated the first grade in nearby Huntington. There an unfortunate accident occurred. Running though the snow, he darted in front of a car, was hit, and was nearly killed. The snow and a thick snowsuit helped absorb the impact, but the boy was badly injured. The accident not only deformed his jaw and teeth, but it left physical and emotional scars that stayed with him throughout his life.

"He was self-conscious about his jaw and teeth," Louella said. "He would come home from school crying because kids would make fun of him."

By the time Bobby Joe reached the fourth grade, he and his mother had settled once again in South Florida. Soon they were joined by Louella's mother and three sisters and seven of Bobby Joe's cousins. The five adults and eight children shared a five-bedroom house in north Miami Beach.

More people meant more expenses, and Louella started working double shifts at a Lum's Restaurant to pay the bills. Of course this reduced Bobby Joe's private time with her, and soon he felt neglected and resentful. The extra work still did not bring in enough money, so Louella found a higher-paying job mixing drinks at Big Daddy's Lounge.

Her new job required her to wear sexy little outfits that Bobby Joe especially resented. Louella's mother, a strict Baptist, also protested.

Louella remembers Bobby Joe's attitude at this time. "He started being very abusive to me verbally and treating me like filth," she said. "When I tried to explain how much we needed the money, he told me to dress and act like a mother. He said he was hurt and embarrassed."

When the boy was twelve, Louella was able to buy a small stucco home on a quiet street in Hialeah, but her problems continued with her son. School became a growing struggle for Bobby Joe. He would go to school but would soon return home. When the school called to check on him, he would not answer the telephone.

Later, Rudy Machado, a classmate and friend of Bobby Joe's in junior high and high school, characterized these years for police.

"Long was smart but did not make good grades," Machado said. "He was a smart-ass type who never participated in sports or extracurricular activities. He got into a lot of general mischief, but I don't remember him being in trouble with the police."

Machado further stated that he, Long, and another guy named Mike went hunting, fishing, and snorkeling together. He remembered Louella working at Big Daddy's Lounge in Hialeah and having many different boyfriends. Bobby Joe didn't like Louella bringing home different men all the time.

A petite, auburn-haired girl named Cynthia lived within walking distance of Bobby Joe's home. She, like him, was the child of divorced parents, and they soon became fiercely protective of each other. They went everywhere together, fixed meals together, and confided only in each other. They were together constantly, and at night he would sneak into her house.

Louella commented on their relationship: "It was the two of them against the world."

There was another area of confusion for Bobby Joe. He had been born with a genetic disorder that caused unnaturally large breasts in a male.

By the time Bobby Joe had reached adolescence, he had grown to be a large, strong individual. There were minor troubles during his teen years, but nothing of great significance. At fifteen he was accused of stealing a car battery with a friend, but the charge was dropped. At eighteen he was accused of raping a girl, but after he was taken to jail and fingerprinted, he was released when police discovered that the girl had lied. Once, he was issued seven motor vehicle tickets in a single day.

Bobby Joe was never a good student because he refused to study. After he got a part-time job as an electrician's assistant, he dropped out of the tenth grade twice. His third try at the tenth grade ended just after his eighteenth birthday, when the school expelled him for poor attendance.

He and his friend Rudy worked as electricians with Arc Electric in Miami until the company went out of business. He liked the work very much and enlisted in the Army at nineteen so he could become an electrician specialist. He did so well during basic training at Fort Jackson, South Carolina, that he earned a commendation.

His preenlistment contract with the Army called for Bobby Joe to be stationed at Homestead Air Force Base, Florida. While there, he finished his work for a high school diploma. After dating for six years, he and Cynthia married in January 1974 at the base chapel. It seemed that his life now was finally gaining stability.

One month later, Bobby Joe's life took a tragic turn.

Seventeen

Bobby Joe jumped on his motorcycle with his paycheck in his pocket and roared down the palm tree-lined street toward the bank. The sky was already darkening with an afternoon shower as he turned onto Dixie Highway. He put his helmeted head down into the wind to gain speed. Suddenly a car hit him full force and sent him flying into the pavement. The impact split his helmet and the bike crashed down on him before it went careening in a different direction.

Help came fast, but he was unaware of it. He was still unconscious when the ambulance screamed up to the emergency entrance at the MacDill Air Force Base hospital. His leg had been crushed so badly that doctors were strongly considering amputation. Finally they decided they might be able to save the leg, so they set it as well as possible and put it in a cast. His head and shoulders were also braced before Cindy was notified.

During the days and weeks that followed, Cindy noticed distinct changes in his behavior. His sex drive had definitely increased, and he was insisting on sexual activity each time she visited him. Nurses reported that in addition to this, he was masturbating four or five times a day.

As the weeks passed and he was allowed to return home, his leg continued to be very painful. This was a condition that was to be with him for many years, in varying degrees of discomfort.

"Since the accident," his father once remarked, "Bobby Joe was like a Jekyll and Hyde. He could be as sweet as could be, and the next minute there would be nothing but anger and shouting."

In his later confession, Long stated that his "classified ad" rapes started after his release from the hospital. Also a few months after his release, in August of 1974, Long was discharged from the Army. The Army refused to disclose Long's service record, but his wife remembered that he received a medical discharge. Court documents indicated that he received disability checks. He had contested a dishonorable discharge and an Army lawyer had gotten it changed to a general discharge.

The Longs began civilian life living in a trailer in the Honey Hill Trailer Park in Carol City, Florida. Cindy tried to cope with her new situation by working full-time as a secretary, even though she was now pregnant. Bobby Joe could find only odd jobs of short duration. He utilized his GI benefits and attended Broward Community College to study radiology, which would allow him to get a better paying job.

Continued shortage of money, however, sometimes resulted in bitter arguments between the couple, and their verbal abuse progressed to physical violence. Cindy was a tough survivor. She said that whenever he hit her she'd hit him back. Afterward, she recalled, he'd always apologize.

Before their first year of marriage had passed, a blond son was born. Early the next year, she became pregnant again and decided that things might be better if they had a larger place. They moved to 133rd Avenue in Fort Lauderdale, where a daughter was born in 1975.

Prior to Christmas, 1975, Long went to West Virginia to search for a job. He liked electrical work, but the old leg injury made that type of work difficult. After a week or two, he returned home with presents for the children.

Frustrated and restless, the Longs moved three times during 1976. Their last move was to a three-bedroom cinderblock home in South Hollywood, Florida, which they purchased. Louella and Joe Long helped them buy the house. They were now living together in Kenova, West Virginia, where Joe worked at an automobile factory.

Bobby Joe continued to attend Broward Community College classes during the day while working evenings at the area hospital radiology departments in X-ray-related jobs. Cynthia continued working as a secretary. When both were occupied, neighbors cared for the children.

One baby-sitter said that Long gave her the creeps. "He always liked to grab you and hug you," she said, "and lay you down—stuff like that."

Eventually, Long was awarded an associate degree from Broward Community College in X-ray technology. In November of 1979, he took his first X-ray technician job at Parkway Medical Center in north Miami Beach.

Neighbors recall that Cynthia and Bobby Joe were not a compatible couple. He would repeatedly stay home while she went out with friends. One neighbor said that Cynthia liked to party a lot, and consequently, when she filed for divorce from Bobby Joe in June of 1980, few were surprised.

After the divorce was granted, Long moved to an apartment in Fort Lauderdale. Restless, he visited Rudy Machado in Ocala for a few days, returned to Miami, where he lost his job at the hospital, and finally moved to Tampa. There he leased an efficiency apartment in Sulphur Springs.

Susan Replogle, Rudy's pretty sister-in-law, whom Long had met at a wedding, called him. She wanted to know if Long would be interested in sharing an apartment with her in Tampa. She needed help with the rent and explained that they would be working opposite shifts. He decided to move in with her, but it didn't work since Susan also had a child living with her. She did, however, decide to help Long with another arrangement by calling her old boyfriend, Ted Gensel.

Long had previously met Gensel and considered him compatible, and they agreed to split rent on a three-bedroom house on Meadowbrook Drive in Forest Hills. Soon Susan and her child moved in with them. She recalled that they were all friends together and shared interests in water sports and barhopping at the Dallas Bull and Faces Lounge.

"Bobby Joe didn't drink much," recalled Susan. "He didn't smoke, either, or do drugs."

What he did do was work at local jobs, ride his bicycle, play racquetball, and participate in all water recreation, such as scuba diving, swimming, and fishing. He also told friends that he was taking karate and boxing lessons. During 1980 and 1981 Long visited Rudy Machado in Ocala several times. They went deer hunting in the fall and fishing in the summer, just as they had done since high school.

Long and Susan Replogle parted company bitterly. She had accused Long of raping her, but police considered the evidence insufficient to prosecute the charge. They had a physical confrontation two weeks later, when, Susan said, Long punched her in the face and threw her out the door during an argument. She filed a misdemeanor battery charge against Long in October of 1981.

On November 17, 1981, Long pleaded "No Contest" to exhibiting obscene material to a twelve-year-old Tampa girl. He sent her an obscene letter and three obscene photographs. He was caught when police traced telephone calls to his house. A county judge sentenced him to two days in jail and six months' probation for the misdemeanor.

Eighteen

Long's life was as out of control as a run-away train, so in January of 1982, he decided to go back to his parents' home in Kenova to try to get a handle on things.

One foggy night he learned the lesson of his criminal life when there was a knock at the door. His father opened the door, startled to find two young men with guns standing there. They pushed their way in, slammed the door shut, and thoroughly bound the couple with rope. They watched helplessly as their house was casually robbed by thieves before they slowly departed. Ironically, Bobby Joe, who was hiding in his bedroom watching all this, saw how this style of binding a captive controlled them completely. This lesson left a lasting impression. He used bondage many times in the years that followed. Consoling his shaken parents that night, all he could manage was to untie them and verbally attack the robbers as scummy low-lifes.

During the bitter cold of the remaining West Virginia January, Bobby Joe made up his mind to go to California. There, in Wilmington, he enrolled in a commercial diving course that he completed in September. His classmates there remembered him as a redneck and a braggart, apparently much like the others in his school. On completing the course, he once again went back to his parents' home and spent the fall sending out applications for diving jobs. There simply were none available, and for months he sat at home. He seldom went out. He brooded a lot, spoke little to his parents, and spent his time watching television. No one could reach him. "He'd break your heart," his father sighed. "Not for the things he said, but for the things he didn't say."

Finally in February of 1983, Bobby Joe got a temporary job at the Huntington Veterans Administration Hospital. Lea Anne Caines, chief X-ray technologist and Long's supervisor, said that he was a good worker. He was polite and sometimes joined his co-workers after work for drinks. Long was very friendly with one girl at work and he drove her to Tampa around Easter 1983. They vacationed for six days together while he looked for work there. When they returned to West Virginia, Bobby Joe was hired full-time in the radiology department at Huntington Hospital. He was fired after four weeks for instructing women to undress unnecessarily. He did not protest the firing.

He went back to Florida and found a week-end job at Humana Hospital in Brandon, just east of Tampa, in July of 1983. Prior to leaving West Virginia, he purchased a 1979 maroon two-door Dodge Magnum with a white interior.

When Long first moved to Brandon, he lived at the Turks Cap Apartments and he often visited Ted Gensel and his new wife, Susie, who lived nearby. At a Fourth of July party at the Gensels', he met a small, green-eyed blonde. They left the party and went to Bobby Joe's apartment, where they had sex. She related that his attitude "turned her off." They returned to the party and never dated again.

About a month later, Bobby Joe met a tall, dark-haired nurse at Humana Hospital named Elise. They started dating in August. Long called home excitedly and told his parents of the new relationship. He said that his new girlfriend was very religious and that when they went out on dates she would witness to people and give them religious pamphlets. Long started attending church with her and it looked like his attitude toward life was improving. He even sent his ex-wife Cynthia $4,000 in back child support.

Trouble, however, was never far away. In September of 1983, Long was found guilty and sentenced to probation in a nonjury trial in the Susan Replogle battery case, which had been filed in October 1981. Long was furious. Acting without a lawyer, he started a letter-writing campaign to clear his name.

He wrote several letters to County Judge Robert H. Bonanno. Long's letters were detailed and explicit. He asserted, "I'm no angel, but as I said before, I did nothing criminal."

He attacked Susan Replogle in his letters, citing her arrest for indecent exposure as a topless dancer on Nebraska Avenue. He felt that her innocent appearance had influenced the judge in the first trial. Long demanded and was given a new trial.

At the second trial in early 1984, Long was represented by an attorney. Among the neighbors who testified against him was Hugh Connor, who said that he saw Long strike Replogle. Connor warned the court that Long was a violent man. The jury acquitted Long, however, and he laughed at the victim as he left the courtroom.

Long continued his job at Humana. When the girl he had met at the Gensels' Fourth of July party moved out, Bobby Joe moved back into their house on Meadowbrook. Long continued to date Elise from Humana.

* * *

March 6, 1984. A woman who advertised her home for sale was raped and robbed in Port Richey, FL.

Long abruptly quit his job at Humana Hospital on March 30, 1984. During the spring and summer months, Bobby Joe gave Elise a lot of good jewelry. She asked how he could afford it since he was not working, but his answers were evasive.

In April, Bobby Joe moved into an apartment near Dale Mabry and Waters, and he applied for a job as X-ray technician at Tampa General Hospital on April 3. Two days later, he abducted a woman in the Jaguar. Later in the month he called home and told his mother that he'd caught Elise seeing another man. His mother recalled that Bobby Joe was especially upset because Elise's new friend had a "filthy" bumper sticker slogan on his truck. Louella recalled that he seemed broken-hearted and lost. He said to her, "Mom, I can't find any decent girls in the world. They've all gone bad."

Things just got worse. Long went to work as an electrician for Gulf Bay Electric in Tampa from May 3 until May 23, 1984. His supervisor, Chad, remembered that Long talked very crudely about girls. He reported that Bobby Joe spoke to him about watching porno movies with girls fourteen and sixteen years old, and said they all tried to duplicate the sex acts they saw in the films. Long carried a lot of nude pictures in his wallet. Once in a while on the job, he stared at a girl walking down the street and said, "How would you like to bend that one over and make her squeal like a pig?" Long then said, "I'd like to give it to her right up her ass!"

May 4, 1984. Lana Long murdered.
May 26, 1984. Michelle Simms murdered.
May 29, 1984. Classified Ad rape/robbery in Pinellas County.
June 8, 1984. Elizabeth Loudenback murdered.

During early June, Bobby Joe visited his wife and children and stayed overnight with them. On June 14, Long started a job at Tampa General Hospital. He worked Thursday through Sunday each week for ten hours a day as an X-ray technician.

July 4, 1984. Long's ex-mother-in-law called Lady Lake Police Department when Long argued over seeing his son in her custody.
July 17, 1984. Long received fine and probation in the April abduction.

* * *

On July 24, Long bought furniture for a new apartment on East Fowler Avenue, located above a strip mall. He returned on July 29 and purchased a recliner, an end table, and a coffee table. All the items were delivered to Fowler Avenue on August 7.

During this summer, Bobby Joe took a trip to Miami, where he picked up a prostitute and drove her to a remote area to the west. There he beat her with his fists and forced her to undress. He then took pictures of the girl bent over the reclined front seat while he was raping her. The pictures were graphic close-ups of sexual acts being performed in every way imaginable. The pictures were found in Long's apartment and were positively identified by an envelope seen between the seats of his car which clearly bore his name and address. He had allowed this girl to go free, kicked out of his car nude in an isolated area.

September 7, 1984. Vicky Marie Elliott murdered.

The second week in September, Bobby Joe visited Cynthia and his children again. He was there two days and spent the night at their house. After he returned to Tampa, he was told on September 27 that he'd been fired from Tampa General because he lacked the advanced certification needed for the job.

Long's co-workers at Tampa General from June through September of 1984 gave detailed reports when interviewed. Generally, he was reported to be an average employee who was competent in his field. His weekend supervisor in radiology was Eugene DiBetta. DiBetta remembered Long talking about girls, fishing, diving, hunting, and football. He stated that Long played a lot of racquetball at the University of South Florida. Among the things that bothered DiBetta were Long's comments of a sexual nature to female employees. He said Long told him about dating Elise, a born-again Christian. Long said they were trying to straighten out their problems and get back together again.

Another person Long dated from Tampa General was Ruth Allende, a short brunette. Their first date was in early September. They dated several times, doing routine things like dinner, movies, and sunbathing at the pool. After several dates, Long spent the night with her and they had normal sexual relations.

After his termination from Tampa General, they kept in telephone contact. The last conversations that they had were on November 11 and 13.

Patricia Dunne, an X-ray staff technician,

stated that Bobby Joe talked about sex too
much and related everything to it. She felt
uncomfortable, nervous, and intimidated
around him. He would ask for dates in a
teasing manner, but she added that he was
very sociable and competent in his job and
that his attitude toward patients was good.

Berry Lashawn reported that she and
Bobby Joe got along pretty well and normally watched football on weekends when
possible. He was a Miami Dolphins fan. She
stated that he did kid around a lot about sex
and was preoccupied with the subject. His
comments about women were consistent with
street language, and he and she did not so-
cialize off duty. She said that Long had a
"short fuse" at times.

Several co-workers characterized Long as a
man who had good job skills but was lazy.
They thought he was superficial, too. They
all reported that he did not react well to female supervision.

David Dray quoted Long as liking strip
joints and topless bars and as saying that
women who worked in such places were better at sex than "nice" girls. Long told a
friend that he liked to go to the Sly Fox and
the Library Lounge and talk and flirt with
bar girls. He said, "I like bad girls and I
like to fuck them in the ass." The man said
he thought Long was a big bullshitter and
always had sex on his mind.

September 30, 1984. Chanel Williams murdered.
October 7, 1984. Kimberly Hopps murdered.
October 13, 1984. Karen Dinsfriend murdered.

On October 16, 1984, Bobby Joe drove to visit Cynthia and the children once again. As usual, he spent the night and returned home the next day.

November 3-4, 1984. Lisa McVey kidnapped and raped.
November 10, 1984. Kim Swann murdered.

On November 13 or 14, Long played racquetball with Charles Gaines in a pick-up game at USF. Gaines, when interviewed by the task force, said that he usually played four or five times a month and that Long was one of several good players who often had informal matches. He found Long to be a nice guy who had a good attitude even when he lost but who sometimes got frustrated with himself. Gaines had known Long for a year and a half and knew that he worked as a hospital technician and was divorced. He thought that Long's comments about women were normal in a group of men. He described Long's arrest as unbelievable.

* * *

Just as the city had become mesmerized with every terrifying account of the serial murders, now, after Long's arrest, they wanted to know every mundane aspect of the man's life. The media tried to meet this need by interviewing anyone they could find who had ever had contact with him. The public's appetite for this information seemed insatiable.

Among the first people contacted were Long's neighbors at the apartment complex on Fowler Avenue. This two-story building was on the corner of a busy roadway and had four businesses downstairs below the six apartments.

Downstairs neighbors at the hair salon said that Long complained frequently about the noise when the beauty shop was being remodeled.

"I'll tell you this for certain," said a stylist. "If we'd known he was up *there*, we would not have been down *here*."

Conversely, a maintenance worker at the complex said that Long was very quiet and seemed to mind his own business. "I never saw anybody with him. That's the funny thing about this."

"I'd say he was just an average person," said David Bekiempie, manager of the group that owned the apartment building. "I would never have suspected that he had committed these crimes that he's accused of. He seemed like a pleasant person.''

Nineteen

On November 27, 1984, Hillsborough County Circuit Judge John P. Griffin listened to both sides at a court hearing to determine if the Long case should be presented to the grand jury. Public Defender Charles J. O'Connor represented Bobby Joe Long. He told the judge that news coverage of the murders both before and after the arrest had prejudiced the public, and possibly the grand jury, against his client. O'Connor asked the judge to block the indictment in Hillsborough and move the case to another county. If this was not possible, O'Connor requested that each juror be interviewed about his or her impressions of the case as received from news reports.

O'Connor charged that law enforcement officials acted in concert with the press to release information suggesting Long's guilt to the public. O'Connor read statements from a stack of *Tampa Tribune* newspapers that he said were inflammatory.

Assistant State Attorney Michael L. Benito

told the judge that O'Connor's argument was woefully lacking. Benito argued that there is no constitutional right to an unbiased grand jury. A grand jury decides only whether probable cause exists to make a charge. They do not decide whether a defendant is guilty beyond a reasonable doubt. Benito closed by stating that O'Connor's motion was insulting to the members of the grand jury in implying the jury would be biased as a result of media coverage.

Judge Griffin thanked both sides and said he would consider legal precedents, the attorney arguments, and the media exhibits before making a ruling in the morning.

On Wednesday, November 28, 1984, at nine A.M., Judge Griffin ruled against Long and directed that the grand jury hear the case against him. Dets. Baker and Latimer and Lt. Terry effectively presented the case against Long of murder, nine counts of abduction, the rape of Lisa McVey, and the probation violation in the Jaguar assault case.

One week later, on December 5, the same arguments were repeated in Pasco County. Assistant Public Defender Robert Norgard filed four motions in Pasco County Circuit Court asking that grand jury proceedings against Long be moved because of recent publicity. Other motions requested permission to question potential grand jury jurors and to have a court reporter transcribe proceedings for future use in Long's defense.

Assistant State Attorney Robert P. Cole argued that the county public defender's office had been wrongfully appointed to represent Long. Cole said, "Judge, basically, this court does not have Mr. Long in custody." Cole charged that "The public defender has made allegations that he [Long] was charged in Pasco County. That is entirely false, and I believe that is what Judge Cobb based his appointment on."

Circuit Judge Lawrence E. Keough said the proper time for Norgard to raise his objections would be after the Pasco grand jury was empaneled, but before it had been sworn. He would not comment on the appointment of the public defender to represent Long. The judge recommended the attorneys settle that issue before the grand jury convened.

On December 7, Judge Keough empaneled the Pasco County grand jury. Before the jury was sworn in, Norgard, representing Long, challenged the grand jury's empanelment. In a whispered meeting of attorneys before the bench, the judge made several rulings. He turned down Norgard's attempt to block the grand jury from handling Long's case. The judge did grant the motions requesting a court reporter to transcribe the proceedings and the judge agreed to question jurors about the effect of media accounts of the case. Two jurors were excused after they indicated they were biased against Long. A young man and a young woman both admitted having prejudices.

The grand jury was sworn to serve a term until the first Tuesday of the following April. The thirteen men and five women then heard the evidence and indicted Long on one count of first-degree murder in the death of Virginia Lee Johnson, an eighteen-year-old native of Danbury, Connecticut.

As soon as Long was indicted, his appointed defense attorneys requested a series of psychological, neurological, and intelligence tests. Each required a written request through the court which was compiled with the help of the remaining members of the HCSO task force.

The examinations took place in 1985 and 1986. Psychiatrist Dr. Michael Maher was appointed by the court to evaluate Bobby Joe Long, and he immediately gathered information about Long's childhood. He discovered that Long's mother had mental illness on her side of the family, and the doctor believed that both of Long's parents were mentally ill themselves. In his opinion, Long's relationship with his mother did not develop in a positive, healthy manner.

His conclusions were that Long had psychiatric illness from three sources. First, there was the inherited genetic risk factor present at birth. The second factor was his environment as he developed from child to young adult. Third were the brain injuries when Long was seven years old and in the later motorcycle accident. Dr. Maher said that Long had an affective disorder and an organic brain impairment and in his opinion was under the influence of extreme mental or emotional disturbance. Long's capacity to conform to the requirements of law was massively diminished and his capacity to appreciate the criminality of his acts was diminished. However, Dr. Maher said that Long knew what he was doing was wrong and although he might not be insane legally, he was medically.

After a competency examination of Long, Maher found him competent to stand trial and able to assist his counsel, and stated that Long knew right from wrong. Maher reviewed the police records and confessions and Long acknowledged committing eight or nine murders and rapes in those cases and at least a half dozen others.

In his testimony, Maher produced VA hospital records from 1974 to 1984, including the motorcycle accident claim. Prolific correspondence by Long was found in those files, and letters showed that he thought his claim for money was justified.

Maher's notes also reflected Long's history,

including Los Angeles rapes in 1982. Long
reported that many times a victim willingly
submitted and enjoyed it. These victims were
aged twelve to forty. Long was attracted to
very young girls in a way that was pathologi-
cally sick, and Maher was sure that Long had
lied to him during his discussions. There was
no question that Long lied regularly and
consistently and had for his entire life. He
had little regard for the truth even when he
could determine what it was. Maher was absolutely sure that Long had committed murder and many rapes. Long described how
he'd killed various victims, and Maher added
that it was no coincidence that most were
prostitutes. Some were raped but not killed.
Lisa McVey was not a prostitute and he had
let her go. A conscious decision had been
made not to kill her.

Maher agreed with Cindy's observation
that Long thought everybody owed him. As
a child he had tormented animals. His pattern of behavior was that he thought about
ways in which he hurt his victims and he
injured them both psychologically and emo-
tionally. Maher believed that in some cases
Long derived sick pleasure from knowing he
was hurting people, while others were the
playing-out of simple fantasies. The doctor
believed the two were mixed together in
Long's report to him.

This was the first serial killer with whom

Dr. Maher had spoken, but he said other people had bad childhoods, motorcycle accidents, and head injuries and didn't become serial killers. An abnormal EEG did not prevent one from becoming a lawyer or a scientist or a judge. Long's IQ was normal, but his perception of himself was very distorted and self-centered. Maher said that the statement "It doesn't bother me a bit to kill someone" sounded like Bobby Joe Long. Long mentioned in a letter about having arresting officers killed and having hit men do them in. He also wanted to delay judicial proceedings, aware that psychiatric testimony might be useful in his defense. He did not believe that one of the motivations in killing the women was not to leave witnesses.

When Dr. Robert Berland, a forensic psychologist, was appointed to evaluate Long, he determined that Long had two kinds of psychotic disturbance: first, an inherited bipolar or manic-depressive psychosis; and, second, an organic brain syndrome caused by damage to brain tissue. The second psychosis may have been caused by Long's accident at age twenty, or his chronic amphetamine abuse following the motorcycle accident.

Dr. Berland said that in addition to the psychoses, Long had two nonpsychotic diagnoses: an antisocial personality disorder, and paraphilia. Paraphiliacs share common backgrounds that include a very disorganized family situation with a dominant, controlling, capricious, sometimes violent mother and a weak, passive father. Family life is characterized by chaos, frequent movement, alcohol abuse, sexual promiscuity, and parental negligence alternating with control over petty matters. Men with antisocial personality disorder and paraphilia typically take out their anger against women by raping or otherwise demeaning them. The combined effect of a bipolar disorder causing hypersexuality and a paranoia causing rage produced an irrationally, sometimes bizarrely and poorly controlled mental disorder with anger toward women as its focus.

During trial testimony, Berland said that Long had the background of a sexual offender and that his background influences predated his motorcycle accident.

Long said that he hated women and derived pleasure from their pain and that he loved to destroy people. Dr. Berland found Long to be a manipulator with a character disorder and thought he was dangerous. With an IQ of 118, which is above average, Long appreciated the criminality of his acts.

Dr. John Money was a specialist in psychoendochrinology, dealing with hormones in sexology. He contacted Long in August of 1987 and used the letters that they wrote to each other as diagnostic tools. He also had a telephone call with Long's mother, and on the morning of Berland's testimony, he had an interview with Long.

He said that Long was a paraphiliac and was in a Jekyll-and-Hyde fugue state. Dr. Money believed that society should do research on Long, who had written to him with interest in finding out what was wrong.

He had evaluated Long and diagnosed a paraphilia called "sexual sadism," a brain disorder which caused his criminal behavior. Dr. Money also diagnosed temporal lobe epilepsy, a peculiar kind of epilepsy that does not cause seizures but that causes one to enter an altered state of consciousness, and another overlapping syndrome, manic-depressive disorder. He said that all paraphiliacs, to a certain degree, have paranoid thinking and a schizophrenic preoccupation with ideas and obsessions that "won't give up." The doctor said that Long, by the very nature of his condition, had "antisocialism." Dr. Money said that a head injury could be 100 percent responsible for sexual sadism. Long had had five head injuries between the ages of three and nine. The major one, however, was in a motorcycle accident when Long was twenty. That head injury, which left him unconscious, was the source of brain damage that could have produced paraphilia. The onset of epilepsy in the brain might also have produced paraphilia. Dr. Money concluded that his diagnosis of Long was sexual sadism (a paraphilia) and dual personality phenomenon, neither of which Long could control.

When clinical psychologist and neuropsychologist Dr. Sidney Merin was asked to evaluate Bobby Joe Long, he already had Long's letters regarding his escape and his plans to murder investigating officers. When he gave Long a neuropsychologist test, he found his verbal IQ was 120 and the composite IQ was 118. He was not able to discuss the murders with Long, but Merin diagnosed him as an antisocial personality free of significant impairment of the brain.

He found Long to be bright, but with an obsessive type of personality, a man who thinks a great deal. He did not believe Long to be psychotic nor to have the emotional turmoil to justify a neurosis diagnosis. Dr. Merin repeated that Long was an antisocial personality and was not under the influence of extreme mental or emotional disturbance, and his capacity to appreciate the criminality of his conduct was not impaired. He described Long's anger, bitterness, and vengeful attitude. He believed Long to be a manipulator and a very dangerous serial killer.

Psychiatrist Dr. Daniel Sprehe interviewed Long, looked at his prison records, and examined his VA file. He examined Long for three hours in 1985, gave him a clinical psychiatric exam and a clinical psychological interview, and found no problems. He found Long to be clear and very bright, with a high IQ. Long discussed the murders of Johnson, Long, Simms, Swann, Elliott, Hopps, Dinsfriend, Loudenback, and Williams, and also said he committed other rapes. The doctor found Long to have a longstanding severe antisocial personality disorder and to be competent. He felt Long knew exactly what he was doing and was clearly able to control himself at those times. There was no extrinsic evidence whatsoever that he was psychotic, nor under the influence of extreme mental or emotional disturbance, and his capacity to appreciate the criminality of his conduct was not substantially impaired.

Dr. Sprehe said Long displayed anger at women and was a very good manipulator and proud of his talent as a con artist. He also believed that Long was a real escape risk and a dangerous serial killer. Long told Sprehe that one reason for Long's killing these women was to remove witnesses.

When psychiatrist Dr. Arturo Gonzalez examined him, Long told the doctor of many rapes. Gonzalez diagnosed him as an antisocial personality, not psychotic, having mental illness. He also believed that Long was not under any extreme mental or emotional disturbance and that he could appreciate the criminality of his acts. He described Long as

a manipulator and said it was apparent
throughout the records and letters that he
had written. Dr. Gonzalez said that Long was
a very dangerous individual, not a sadist
type, and that he had the ability to make
choices and to act upon them.

Dr. Dorothy O. Lewis, Professor of Psychia-
try at NYU Medical Center, communicated
to Long's current attorney, Ellis S. Rubin,
that Long had a history of multiple severe
head injuries. At about four or five years of
age, Long told Lewis that he'd fallen off a
swing, was knocked unconscious, and awak-
ened to find a stick still stuck in his left
eyelid. He also said he'd suffered a bicycle
injury at age five or six, and at age seven,
was hit in the face with the bumper of a
car, knocked unconscious, lost several teeth,
and was hospitalized in West Virginia. At
about age eight, he said, he was thrown from
a pony. In third grade, he fell from a fence,
injured the left side of his head, and required stitches.

Probably the most serious head injury occurred in March of 1974, when Long had a
motorcycle accident in which his motorcycle
hit a car; he was thrown from the motorcycle, and he suffered a skull fracture. Long
told Lewis he was hospitalized for a long
time and said that it was after the accident
his sexual appetite increased greatly and that
he required sex with his wife twice a day,

when previously, it had been two or three times a week.

Lewis suggested that Long's very first sexual assault occurred while he was still in a partial cast.

Twenty

The task force continued to function with limited HCSO assistance to support the preparation of the cases as a result of the Long indictments. Numerous requests from the state prosecutors and appointed defense lawyers were handled. In addition, the continuing FBI analysis of the last victim's evidence and numerous requests from other law agencies generated many hours of extra work.

Steve Cribb spent most of the day on December 5 working with the tapes of the Long confession taken by Latimer and Price on the evening of November 16. He removed the tapes, stored under inventory 37810, item 5, and took them to the Hillsborough Community College Ybor campus audiovisual room. There he made copies for the state attorney's office and the public defender representing Long. When Cribb had finished, he took the originals back to the evidence room before delivering the extra copies.

The next day, Cribb contacted Sgt. Pell of

County Jail Central, where Bobby Joe Long was being held. She reported that Long had received several packages from his parents. Two hardback books had been retained, magazines not allowed in the cell had been kept as well, and some checks had been returned to his parents. Everything was carefully monitored. One week before, he had received a package of clothing containing shorts, T-shirts, and handkerchiefs. His mail included copies of search warrants from Captain Diecidue and a letter from Doug Hoyer of Channel 10 News. Gary Terry asked for a shakedown of Long's cell, but nothing suspect was revealed.

Long met with his lawyers on December 7 on the third floor of County Jail Central. His Hillsborough lawyer, Charles O'Connor, and his Pasco lawyer, Norgard, met with Det. Cribb and ID Technician Wilson. Two sets of major case prints were made of Long. One was for the FBI, the second for HCSO.

Three days later, on December 10, a meeting was held by HCSO for all interested law enforcement agencies to help them in identifying Bobby Joe Long as a possible suspect in open cases. The task force team supplied information on Long to law enforcement representatives in areas where Long had lived and visited.

Due to recent criticism of media coverage by Long's lawyers, few details of the meeting were released. Greg Bigler, a Miami detective, did say that a lot had been learned about Long but that it was still too early to link him with certain Miami area investigations. Greg Smith of the Metro-Dade Police Department agreed, but called the meeting "very informative."

Several days were spent attempting to track down the manufacturer of the vehicle carpet and the specific dye used in order to help the FBI fiber unit in their analysis. A series of telephone calls routed them from the local Chrysler-Plymouth dealer to the southeastern district manager for Chrysler in the United States to Chrysler Corporation in Detroit, Michigan. There it was determined that the carpet in a nonconsole vehicle was installed under production number M683 and purchased from the C. H. Maslin Carpet Company in Michigan and their address was given. This company wove the yarn into the rug and dyed the color into the material. They supplied the dye formula so it could be used in matching tests using spectrographic analysis at the FBI.

The trail then led to Candlewick Yarn in Georgia under the number 2/1cc NTG BRT 18d Style 7167 NAT 4.0(Z). They reported that the yarn used by Maslin was made from 100 percent Star Fiber nylon. This is a type 6 nylon, type number 2990, 18-denier size crimpset fiber. This fiber was used from May 5, 1976 through October 30, 1979. The company stated that 597,000 pounds were shipped in 1979.

All this data was sent to special agent Michael Malone in the FBI fiber analysis lab to support his exact identification of the fiber evidence.

On December 13, a white blouse was removed from the property room. This blouse had been thrown out by Long prior to his arrest but had been recovered from the dumpster by the surveillance team after his arrest. This item was sent sealed via UPS to the FBI lab for analysis.

Lee Baker contacted the New York State Police on December 14 in reference to Long's canceled check to a company suspected of developing and printing the lewd photographs taken by Long of a Miami prostitute in his car. This series of explicit pictures helped to explain how Long had raped his victims in the reclined right front seat. The company in question, which was under investigation by the State of New York, was unable to provide additional information.

The week prior to Christmas, Baker and Cribb spent most of their time coordinating the security and escorting Long to medical examinations and tests in the Tampa-Saint Petersburg area. During the holidays, more than a dozen agencies requested and were sent data on Long for their investigations.

In early January, Long requested specific clothing from Property to be placed at the county jail for his upcoming court appearances. His letter was put in the property file and the clothing was photographed and transferred as requested.

On January 4, Elise, the nurse, was located in Ohio and interviewed by telephone. She reported that she would be returning to the area by the end of the month and would contact the task force when she arrived. Also on this day, Lee Baker contacted Sheriff Griffin's office in Russell County, Alabama. Located in well-known Phoenix City, they had two open murder investigations from February of 1983 and August of 1984. Both were strangulations similar to those done by Bobby Joe Long. Griffin's office requested a background package on Long to review prior to sending a detective over later in the month. Baker prepared the information and sent it out.

Mike Malone called on January 10 with an eagerly awaited conclusive report. Fibers found from the Loudenback evidence confirmed Bobby Joe's confession. Hair from both Lana Long and Karen Dinsfriend was found in Bobby Joe's car, and the tire impressions from the Lana Long and Simms evidence positively compared with the tires from Bobby Joe's vehicle. A satisfied Malone promised to mail the complete report.

Det. Bigler of Metro-Dade in Miami called on January 15 in reference to the Glades County case. He had found the woman in Long's lewd photographs. She was in a hospital in Miami after having been severely beaten by her pimp. Bigler said he planned to interview her.

Then, on January 18, Lee Baker got a phone call from TPD's Sgt. Bob Price, asking him to come over immediately. Baker met Price in his office and was introduced to Richard Powell, a licensed private investigator, who had quite an interesting story to tell.

Powell told the officers how an inmate in HCSO central jail had contacted him three times during the last two months. During the last call, the inmate, Jay R. Scheidler, told him that he had some letters from Bobby Joe Long. Baker leaned forward with interest and Price nodded for the investigator to continue.

"I went to the jail and read the letters," Powell said, "I think Scheidler thought that showing them to me would help him in some way. Anyway, some of the letters talked about a plot to escape, showing diagrams, and also about some plot to kill a girl." The detectives listened intently as Powell continued. "Other letters indicated that Long had drugs stashed in his cell, and others suggested that he might be thinking about suicide."

Powell told them that Scheidler was under the assumption that Powell would be dealing with the state attorney's office, not the police. He said the inmate had visions of making money from the letters and wanted to continue writing to Long to receive more information.

As soon as the interview ended, Baker grabbed the phone and called Gary Terry. Terry and Cribb met with Baker immediately. Terry announced that he would like the letters that day, if possible.

"Let's go," Baker said to Powell, and they drove to the county jail. It was about five P.M. and Powell went in alone, carrying a briefcase. A short time later, he came out, patting the briefcase as he got into the car.

"The letters are in here." He smiled at Baker and they hurried back to TPD, where the others waited. Powell emptied the case on a large table and they all pulled up chairs and began reading. Terry moved quickly, like an animal with a new scent. He contacted the jail for an immediate search for the pills that had been mentioned, and he took all the letters with him. The original letters

were put in Property at HCSO and copies
were made for the state attorneys. Powell was
fingerprinted and signed a property receipt
indicating that he had released the letters to
HSCO.

Two days later, Powell notified Baker that
Scheidler had about ten more pages of letters from Long. The next day they went to
the jail together and again Powell picked up
the letters and gave them and a receipt to
Baker. Baker made copies of the letters and
had a conference with Sgt. Price, Lt. Terry,
and Capt. Miller. They met with Assistant
State Attorney Michael L Benito that afternoon, and he was given copies of all of
Long's letters. It was decided to move Long
from his cell to the infirmary area and to
cease the correspondence between Scheidler
and Long.

The next day Terry, Baker, and Novak met
with Capt. Diecidue, Sgt. Deaton, and Lt.
Miranda at the county jail. Bobby Joe Long
was brought to the infirmary cells and identified a note that he had sent to Latimer.
Terry explained to Long that he was being
placed in this new cell, away from inmates
Jay Scheidler and Arthur Copeland, because
of the letters he had written.

Next, the detectives went to talk to
Scheidler and Copeland, who each signed
consent-to-interview forms. The two detectives searched their cells, and in a search of

Long's old cell, a bag full of correspondence was recovered. In Scheidler's cell there were more letters from Long and a razor blade that was turned over to jail authorities. The letters were put in Property.

Scheidler explained that he was really interested in Bobby Joe and wanted to know what made him "tick." Scheidler said, "Bobby Joe really trusted me like no one else!" He continued to explain how the many letters were passed. Each day Copeland got a newspaper. They would pass notes back and forth in the classified section. Marlboro cigarette boxes were pushed from cell to cell, day or night, to pass drugs or notes. Scheidler admitted that he gave pills to Long, and that Long also bought pills from other inmates.

Scheidler encouraged Long to write a novel. After Long wrote about ten or twelve letters, which Scheidler said were "mostly getting-acquainted stuff," Scheidler started saving them. He said that after reading Long's letter about the rape in Orange County, he felt sick. He also said that if the correspondence had been permitted to continue, he thought Long would have told him about the murders.

When questioned about specifics in the letters, Scheidler answered candidly. He thought the escape plan would work. He related that Bobby Joe called all women "cunts" and said that he was a lost, misunderstood kid. The detectives asked Scheidler why Long had committed the murders. He said that in his letters to Long he had provided sort of a multiple choice of possible reasons:

1. Female did you wrong, you feel inferior, driven by hatred.
2. You had bad experiences with a chick; someone you loved fucked you.
3. You're a kinky sex pervert, had a male or female accomplice, group sex, bondage, maybe it got out of hand and you all killed someone.

Bobby Joe had replied, "You were awful close!"

Scheidler said that he would testify against Long and that he had no intention of helping Long escape. He just wanted to find out what Long had done so he could write a book.

The interview with Arthur Copeland, who was in cell E for first-degree murder, was approved by his attorney. Copeland revealed that Long said that the only way he could escape was to have someone help him while he was out with Price and Latimer for examinations.

Copeland told how Long had written him a letter asking about Florida State Prison.

Long specifically asked about getting drugs
in if he wanted to commit suicide. Replying
by letter, Copeland sent a diagram of Florida
State Prison, including fences, and told Long
the only way to get drugs in would be to put
them "up your ass!"

He said Bobby Joe was a potential threat
to himself and to others, that he hated
women and wanted to "pop their eyes out."
He suggested that Long was starting to regret what he had done. Perhaps more accu-
rately, Long was starting to regret being in
jail.

Twenty-one

Nobody in Dade City could remember such tight security at this placid Pasco County Courthouse, but the difference was that today, serial killer Bobby Joe Long was going to be there. Dates were to be set for his trials on murder, rape, kidnapping, robbery, and burglary charges. Each person entering the courtroom was checked with a hand-held metal-detecting wand. Every purse, briefcase, and camera bag was opened and searched. Normally, security consisted of personal recognition or professional identification, but not today.

The February 11, 1985. hearing started at 8:30 A.M., with Long brought from his holding cell through a side entrance into the courtroom. He had an air of confidence as he casually chatted with his appointed defense attorneys, Robert A. Norgard and Randall Grantham, while they awaited for Circuit Court Judge Ray E. Ulmer, Jr. Three plainclothes deputies sat behind Long, and a uniformed deputy stood nearby with his back to the wall. Television camera crews were actively setting up their equipment even as the proceedings began.

Long's appearance contrasted to the way he'd looked when he was arrested three months earlier. His thick brown hair had apparently not been cut, and he was dressed in faded blue coveralls. Either his attire or his lack of exercise made Long look much heavier. He spoke aloud only once. When Judge Ulmer asked if he was Bobby Joe Long, he replied crisply, "Yes, sir."

During the brief hearing, Long watched with cool detachment as his lawyer entered innocent pleas to all charges. He seemed almost preoccupied as trial dates were set for April 15 on the Port Richey rape and April 22 on the murder charge.

Mechanically, Judge Ulmer heard the standard motions filed in death penalty cases attacking the Florida death penalty. Many of Norgard's motions were similar and repetitive, and the judge turned down thirteen of them. Assistant State Attorney Robert Cole did not bother to argue, stating that these motions had been settled by higher courts. At one point, he said impatiently, "It is a waste of the court's time to go over all the same things we went over an hour and a half ago." Norgard said that he did not think it a waste of time to argue that the death penalty is cruel and unusual punishment.

Ultimately during the two-hour hearing, Judge Ulmer granted a prosecution motion to cancel a pretrial conference scheduled for that Wednesday. He took three defense motions under advisement, all of which involved the grand jury that had indicted Long. Norgard challenged the jury composition on grounds of age and the method used by Judge Keough to determine pretrial influence by media publicity.

On the following day, a special hearing was held before Judge Ulmer. At this hearing, Assistant State Attorney Phillip Van Allen requested an order requiring that Long get his upcoming psychiatric examination done at the jail.

Van Allen's personal courtroom presence was notable. He was tall and lean, with brown hair and brown eyes. Since a hunting accident in Texas when he was shot in the foot, the young lawyer had walked with a cane. He'd learned to use the cane to make his judicial performance very dramatic: raising it to make a point, tapping it to show resolve, or hanging it from his expensive suit pocket to express nonchalance.

The judge listened as he explained that he had information indicating that Long might be planning an escape from Hillsborough County Jail. Simply leaning on his cane, Van Allen outlined Long's plan.

Now believing that he had officers sufficiently in his confidence, Long felt he could arrange a trip out of jail to search for another body. Long would then have a friend place either a twelve-gauge shotgun or a high-powered handgun near the search site. Another plan was to try to escape while visiting his court-appointed psychiatrist in Tampa.

Van Allen concluded, "The risk encountered in transporting Long to and from the doctor's office is a very serious risk, and we ask the court to order that he be examined in the county jail. The statement has been attributed to him that if there's any possible way to get out, he'll do it." Van Allen declined to reveal the source of his information.

Norgard stated that the confidentiality of Dr. Szabo's examinations as well as Long's attorney-client privilege might be compromised by security measures at the jail. "Since the escape problems have surfaced, I've had difficulty communicating with my client in confidence because of the increased security," Norgard said. He added that new procedures required Long to be interviewed by the psychiatrist in a room with an open door and with four officers within earshot. He asked that he be given access to the evidence concerning Long's alleged escape plans and said he would not oppose a court order to have his client examined at the jail.

Van Allen sprang up again. "The reason for concern about visitors to Mr. Long is not just for the security of Mr. Long, but for the security of the visitor. I'm not sure Dr. Szabo might not want to have a guard or two standing around when he talks to Mr. Long."

Judge Ulmer ruled that because of the number of charges lodged against Long and a concern for Long's safety and the safety of others, the accused killer should be examined at the jail. If the psychiatrist found that his examination could not be properly conducted in jail, the court would consider other options.

Hillsborough County Assistant State Attorney Michael Benito confirmed after the hearing that he had notified Van Allen of the escape plan and had requested the examination in jail. Benito noted that Long faced charges and had lawyers in both Hillsborough and Pasco Counties.

"Our concern," said Benito, "is that we do not want to move Long from doctor to doctor at the request of public defenders. It's easier for the doctors to come to him in jail." He declined to comment on the origin of the escape stories, and Maj. David Parsh, jail division commander at HCSO, also declined to comment on the story source. In fact, the task force had learned of the plans in Long's letters to fellow inmate Jay Scheidler.

Two weeks later, the pretrial posturing and motions by public defender Norgard continued. He appeared before Judge Ulmer on February 26 and said that his office needed all letters to the editor, newspaper stories, files, and notes relating to Bobby Joe Long. Norgard requested background information on stories that had appeared in the *Tampa Tribune*, *St. Petersburg Times*, *Clearwater Sun*, and *Pasco News*. He cited several motives.

Norgard needed a complete record of publicity to warrant a change of venue. Hate-mail letters would indicate a formidable depth of feeling against Long and newspapers might have received information on the case which was unknown to police. Finally, the newspapers had extensive data on Long's background and early life in West Virginia that might prove useful to his defense.

Assistant State Attorney Robert Cole argued against the motion, calling it a fishing expedition. "The motion is so broad it's difficult to argue against," he added.

The judge agreed. He also disagreed with some of its premises. Ulmer said, "Public knowledge alone is not a sufficient basis for change of venue. The critical factor is the extent of prejudice or lack of impartiality among potential jurors that accompanies that knowledge. Such questions may be better addressed during the jury selection."

Publicity was a strong issue in several of eleven motions made by Norgard during the hearing. He said, "I've never seen so much pretrial publicity in the entire time I've been in Pasco County."

Cole responded that he'd seen cases with more publicity, but none had had trouble picking a jury. Judge Ulmer agreed with Cole.

Norgard then requested that Pasco County pay for the public defender's office staff to travel to Long's home in West Virginia. "The right to counsel is a meaningless gesture," he said, "if the indigent defendant is denied the working tools for an effective defense."

Van Allen accused Norgard of asking for a carte blanche Pasco County credit card. Attorney William Sestak, representing Pasco County clerk of court Jed Pittman, said that the request was vague and would violate the clerk's responsibility to preaudit money he was required to pay out.

In denying the motion, Judge Ulmer said that the county would be opening a Pandora's box by giving indigent criminals the right to county funding in advance without specifying what they wanted. Ulmer granted Norgard a ten-day extension for giving notice that Long planned to use the insanity

defense, and also the right to see a list of
prospective jurors before the trial. He denied
the right to contact jurors without prior
court approval. He denied other motions to
conduct questionnaires of prospective jurors,
to limit contamination of the jury pool, and
to obtain daily trial transcripts.

Long arrived at the West Pasco Detention
Center at 1:30 A.M., Sunday, April 14. He was
accompanied by a total of six law enforcement officers from Hillsborough and Pasco
Counties. Special security procedures to be
used in the courtroom were discussed by
Maj. Tom Berlinger, PCSO.

"Bobby Joe is probably the highest-risk inmate we have ever had in the history of the
county," Berlinger remarked. "There are a
lot of families in central Florida that are sur-
viving relatives of Long's alleged victims. We
cannot afford to slip up and allow one of
them to make an attempt on Long's life."

The Port Richey rape case was concluded
in three days. Items stolen from the victim's
home and later found in Long's apartment
were entered into evidence. The jury heard
an explicit tape-recorded confession by Long
and then witnessed the victim identify him
as her attacker.

The twenty-one-year-old victim testified
that Long entered her house uninvited as a

potential homebuyer. He grabbed her from behind, threatened her with a gun to her head, and bound her hands behind her back. He covered her eyes with surgical tape and forced her to perform oral sex. He cut her work uniform off and raped her, stuffed stockings in her mouth, and tied her to the bed. After that he ransacked the house, identifying items to steal. He raped her once more before he left. Her description to police regarding her attacker's car matched that of Long's car at the time he was captured.

Predictably, assistant public defender Norgard tried to downplay the stolen article evidence as uncertain, declaring also that the victim saw her attacker only briefly.

The four-man, two-women jury took less than forty minutes to find Long guilty on four counts of sexual battery and single counts of burglary, kidnapping, and robbery. Long displayed no emotion. His victim wept quietly in the gallery, relieved by the verdict.

Later the same day, in Dade City, Judge Ulmer denied defense motions to exclude Long's confession in the Virginia Johnson murder trial and to suppress evidence seized after her arrest. The murder trial would begin on Monday, as scheduled.

The cast of principals and the curious began to gather in courtroom 1 of the Pasco

County Courthouse. Long's dark, wavy hair was closely trimmed and he now had a full mustache. He wore a three-piece navy blue suit, a Calvin Klein white shirt, a light blue tie, and "Porto Fino" soft black leather shoes that he'd requested from his personal property. As he swaggered into the courtroom, he waved to his parents, his ex-wife Cynthia and a few friends and relatives from Kenova, West Virginia. Long occasionally winked at his mother.

Before the trial began, Long's lawyer, Bob Norgard, proposed a plea bargain in Judge Ulmer's chambers. Van Allen turned down the offer, preferring to go for the death sentence.

It took forty-eight minutes to question the first prospective juror. After three days, a jury consisting of eight women and four men was seated, but only after the defense had run out of peremptory challenges.

The trial was short and rather predictable. The state had medical examiners, technicians, and dentists establish the victim's identity. FBI special agent Michael Malone traced fibers and hair from the victims to Long's car. A dramatic moment in the trial came when Long's four-minute taped confession was played. In the confession, he detailed the pickup, rape, and murder.

Although his defense team had subpoenaed five witnesses, they decided to present no defense, opting instead for first and last closing statements. In their closing arguments, both Norgard and Grantham said the state had failed to prove premeditation. There was no prosecution reference to Long's motivation or emotional state. No evidence was presented to establish just where and when Long had killed Virginia Johnson, they said.

In his closing argument, Van Allen said strangulation was itself evidence of premeditation. "The hands or the garrotte go around the neck of the victim and you hold and you hold and you squeeze until the victim is dead. Anytime you want the victim to live, you let go. He took her to a desolate, isolated rural country area, bound and naked. He took her clothes when he left. Is there evidence of premeditation?" Van Allen rapped his cane. "It screams!"

Van Allen mentioned that several jurors had referred to Bobby Joe during jury selection as a nice-looking man.

"I submit to you, ladies and gentlemen," Van Allen said, looking directly at Long, "that there is the last face Virginia Johnson saw before she died. While he might be a nice-looking young man, the evidence will show that his is the face of a murderer."

It took the jury just forty-four minutes to

reach their unanimous verdict of guilty. Long, who had displayed no emotion throughout the trial, remained unemotional as the verdict was read. Joe and Louella Long and Cindy were barred from the courtroom, since they were potential witnesses in the sentencing phase. Court reconvened the next day and the jury returned to the courtroom for the penalty phase of the trial.

Van Allen was brief. The state placed in evidence information on the crime and the guilty judgment against Long. Two witnesses were called to present aggravating factors in favor of the death penalty. Raymond Palmer, a parole and probation officer, testified about Long's Hillsborough conviction for armed kidnapping in the Jaguar incident. Don Waugh, PCSO, testified about the convictions the previous week for sexual battery, burglary, kidnapping, and robbery. The state rested.

The defense called a series of witnesses, including Long's mother and his ex-wife. They and doctors Maher, Dunne, and Morrison presented a history of Long's head injuries and progressive mental instability. They testified that Long had brain damage and resultant behavioral problems from three sources: birth defects, adolescent experiences, and head injuries.

Norgard said, "When you look at Mr. Long, you see a normal, healthy individual.

But when you talk to him, there is chaos, with no internal order at all. Bobby Joe Long," his lawyer continued, "sought order in his life through killing prostitutes. According to psychiatrists' testimony, jail might provide a similar order for him."

Norgard asked the court to spare Long's life so society could learn more about serial killers and benefit from their mistakes. "To execute this individual would be cruel and inhuman in light of his condition." Norgard concluded, "I'd like to think society has gone further than to execute people with mental problems."

Van Allen said that Long was guilty not only of murdering Virginia Johnson, but of subjecting her to a cruel death. "She was slowly and agonizingly tortured," he said, "and the defense has offered no justification whatsoever for this murder." Attacking the psychiatrists' findings, he said, "I submit to you that they are working under the preconceived idea that anybody who would commit this murder has to be crazy. That simply is not the law."

The jury quickly returned a recommendation of death by the electric chair. Judge Ulmer recessed the court after announcing that May 3, 1985, would be sentencing day.

In a colorful posttrial interview, Norma Barth, a Dade City juror, said, "None of us bought that stuff about Long being mentally ill. We all know people who have tempers, who blow up when things don't make them happy, but they don't go out killing and raping people. I sat there for a week and he didn't look mentally ill to me. I don't doubt that he has some kind of quirk in his head, but I can't think he's mentally ill. He knows exactly what he does and why he does it."

A week later, a somber Judge Ulmer called court to order. He said he had considered arguments for the defense and had read the presentence report on Long. He leaned forward in his black robe and authoritatively pronounced sentence. "Mr. Long, in keeping with my responsibility, I do accept the responsibility of accepting the jury's recommendation. The aggravating circumstances do outweigh any mitigating circumstances. I would suspect any further comments I would make to you, Mr. Long, would fall on deaf ears." Then Judge Ulmer read the formal death sentence and concluded, "May God have mercy on your soul."

Long's face was expressionless, but as he was led from the courtroom, he began to whistle. Reporters shouted questions as he walked to the jail van handcuffed and flanked by police. His eyes scanned them arrogantly, and as he reached the van for his ride back to Hillsborough County, he turned his head as if to spit on them, but instead delivered a disgusting farewell sneer.

Twenty-two

Publicity surrounding the Pasco County death sentence of Bobby Joe Long was unprecedented. Long was still getting frequent coverage a month later in Hillsborough County, where he was scheduled to begin a series of eight first-degree murder trials. They were booked two weeks apart and the public now was strongly vigilante. Long's lawyer, Assistant Public Defender Charles J. O'Connor, wanted a cooling-off period before they began.

"To expect Long to receive a fair trial in the supercharged atmosphere presently prevailing in Hillsborough County," O'Connor said, "is unthinkable." Circuit Judge John P. Griffin granted him a five-month delay before the first trial began.

The Michelle Denise Simms case was moved from June 3 to October 28. The Karen Dinsfriend trial was rescheduled to November 12, and disposition of the remaining six cases would be considered at that time. Prosecutor Benito did not oppose the request and agreed that pretrial publicity might make it difficult to select an impartial jury.

In fact, Mike Benito welcomed the extra preparation time. He was concerned about the eight murder cases ahead of him. When the facts of the Long murders had been made public after his capture, public interest had continued to build.

Benito was a local boy. He was a USF graduate and after graduating from Florida State University Law School in 1978, he had immediately joined the state attorney's office as a prosecutor. He had a direct, confrontational style in court. His career was on a rapid rise. Benito had been made the office murder-one specialist four years before and he had won every case to date. Benito's spirited courtroom manner made good media copy in high-profile cases. His positive reputation as a prosecutor was growing with the public and with his peers.

Benito entered the Bobby Joe Long case on the night of Long's confession. He went to Long's apartment as part of the investigation team. As soon as he had read the confession transcript, Benito feared the liberal Florida Supreme Court would throw out the confession on appeal.

During the delay, Benito decided to take advantage of a unique set of circumstances. Long had just been found guilty and sen-

tenced to death in Pasco County. There was
no doubt that Long had killed the eight
women in the Hillsborough County cases.
Long and his attorneys were well aware of
Mike Benito and his trial record. Long's confessions were ruled admissible in Pasco
County and the Florida Supreme Court had
not yet ruled on the confessions. The FBI
hair, fiber, and tire evidence was strong. The
Pasco County sentencing phase jury had re-
jected the mental impairment argument and
voted for death. The best that the defense
could hope for was to hold the sentence to
life in prison.

Mike Benito thought the situation was ripe
for a plea bargain. He brought in FBI agent
Michael Malone and had him present the
state's evidence in the eight cases to Long
and his attorneys. After reviewing the evidence, Mike Benito looked them directly in
the eyes and pulled his fingers counting each
victim: "I'll come after you on Simms, then
I'll come after you on Dinsfriend, and Long
and Elliott and Swann and Williams and
Loudenback. You know I'll win some. Each
one I win will be used in the next case, and
after a while I'll have a string of convictions
and you'll receive death in each one."

Then Benito offered the Long team a plea
agreement, making it as attractive as possible. Long would plead guilty in all Hillsborough cases and would receive life in all but

Simms. Benito would get one try at the death sentence in the Simms case but could not use the other seven cases in the Simms sentencing phase proceeding. He had given the defense a lot to think about. Benito would not have to overcome the tainted original confession and would have a possible death sentence in Simms. Long would escape seven possible death sentences.

The Florida death sentence procedure was difficult for the Long defense to attack. Florida's sentencing procedure had been approved by the United States Supreme Court in 1976, when the court had held that it provided enough guidance to prevent arbitrary and capricious imposition of death sentences. Attorneys representing defendants facing the death penalty, however, are an inventive and resourceful group. In the mid-1980s new assaults on the death statute were being mounted in Florida and across the country. From a California case, the new tack became the idea of proportionality review. This strategy could possibly help Long's case. If Long would acknowledge his guilt and plead guilty in the remaining cases, he could be shown as being remorseful and saving the state money in trials. Then it could be argued that if he received a life sentence in most of the murders, he should receive

life as a sentence in the one remaining case
because it was no worse, comparatively speaking, than the others. Possibly adopting this
reasoning, Long, through his attorney
O'Connor, did enter a plea agreement in the
eight Hillsborough murder cases, in the
McVey case, and in the Tampa abduction parole violation.

In exchange for Long's plea of guilty in
all Hillsborough cases, the state made this
recommendation to the court: Long would
receive a life sentence without possibility of
parole for twenty-five years in count three of
the Kimberly Hopps case, and two life sentences for counts one and two, concurrent
with each other but consecutive to the term
for count three. He would, in fact, have to
serve a minimum of fifty years before becoming eligible for parole consideration. In
each of the other murders, Lana Long,
Karen Dinsfriend, Vicky Elliott, Kim Swann,
Chanel Williams, and Elizabeth Loudenback,
the state recommended three concurrent life
sentences with count three of the Hopps
case. In the McVey case, life sentences for
all six counts to run concurrent with the
murder sentences were recommended. In the
probation case, the state recommended five
years to run concurrent with the other cases.

In the Michelle Simms case, Long would
plead guilty to all counts and sentence would
be recommended by a sentencing phase jury.

The court would then impose a sentence of life without parole for twenty-five years or death.

The parties further stipulated and agreed on the following:

1. Long waived his right to contest the admissibility of any statements he has given law enforcement and such statements are admissible in the Simms sentencing phase.

2. Long waived his right to contest the admissibility of evidence seized from his car or apartment, and specifically waived his right to contest the knife found at his apartment in the Simms sentencing phase.

3. The parties to the agreement recognize the negotiations may require sentences which depart from guidelines and waive any issues caused by such departures.

4. The court will decide the number of peremptory challenges to the sentencing-phase jury panel.

5. The court will determine the manner of *voir dire* (questioning of potential jurors) of the sentencing-phase jury.

6. The State of Florida shall not rely on Long's guilty pleas as aggravating circumstances in the Simms sentencing phase. The State may rely upon other

convictions of Long previously obtained
in other counties.

7. Sentences imposed in counts one
and two shall run concurrent to those
in count three of the Simms indictment.

The agreement was signed and dated September 23, 1985, by Robert Joe Long,
Charles O'Connor, Lee William Atkinson,
and Michael L. Benito.

After appropriate inquiry in open court,
trial judge John P. Griffin, Jr., on September
23, 1985, found Long guilty and pronounced
sentence as agreed in each case except in the
Simms murder charge, which was set for a
penalty-phase hearing on December 11, 1985.

As Judge Griffin began the jury selection
for the Simms penalty-phase hearing, Long
moved to withdraw from the plea agreement
entered on September 23. Long based his
withdrawal on the unavailability of a crucial
defense witness and a misunderstanding regarding his right to appeal the confession's
admissibility.

Judge Griffin listened to Long intently.
Long explained how Dr. Morrison was the
main key to his defense. He said he had
been advised that Morrison would be there,
which was why he had agreed to the plea
bargain. He further stated that he had not

understood until now that he was giving up all rights to appeal his confession.

Judge Griffin said, "I'm going to grant the defendant's motion to withdraw his previously entered pleas of guilty." The judge explained that the defendant knew that by withdrawing his plea, he laid himself open to eight death sentences. This convinced the judge how serious Long's concern was about the two points he had outlined.

Long's attorney clarified that the court had authorized Long to make an election whether to continue his guilty pleas or to withdraw them. The court agreed, and with the state's consent, granted a twenty-four-hour continuance.

Long's attorney, Norgard, from the Pasco County trial, was present and probably advised Long that the Florida Supreme Court would reverse the Virginia Johnson verdict and throw out the taped confession. This would add importance to the plea agreement.

On the following day, December 12, Long decided not to withdraw his previously entered guilty pleas. The judge conducted a full inquiry of the entire plea agreement with Long in open court. Covering each point, he asked Long if he understood, and each time Long responded, "Yes, sir." Long also reaffirmed his confidence in Charles O'Connor and the public defender's office.

Judge Griffin set a new sentencing hearing for July 9, 1986, and court was adjourned.

A miserably unhappy man waited on Death Row at a Florida State Prison for his sentencing hearing on the Simms case to begin. The more he reflected upon his situation, the more discontented he became. He was very unhappy with his plea agreement in general and with his lawyer O'Connor in particular. When he had been displeased with the verdict on the Susan Replogle case in Tampa, he had written directly to the judge and changed the outcome. He decided to try that again.

Long wrote two letters to Judge Griffin from Florida State Prison. In the first letter, dated February 13, 1986, he told Judge Griffin that he was being railroaded and requested a talk with the judge. "Mr. O'Connor's representation of me in this matter has resembled the prosecution, not the defense," Long said. "He's been confused and frustrated, and I believe that he's completely missed the essence of what's happened here. He just won't accept anything other than what he wants it to be. Let's face it, my life is in your hands. Isn't it only fair that you know the whole story?"

In the second letter to Judge Griffin, dated March 3, 1986, Long said that he'd been wrong to believe Mr. O'Connor when he'd agreed to the plea arrangement. He said that he'd had no chance with O'Connor representing him and that his only hope was with a private attorney. He stated that he had already written to one who had studied the case and had agreed to take it.

Agreeing to become Long's court-appointed lawyer for the state's maximum fee of a mere $3500 was Miami attorney Ellis Rubin.

Twenty-three

When the controversial, highly publicized Miami attorney Ellis Rubin arrived to represent Long at the Simms sentencing, the defense strategy immediately changed. He shocked the court by introducing Long's confession to a tenth murder. The victim was identified as twenty-year-old Artis Ann Wick, who was found six days after Long's initial arrest. This was part of Rubin's plan to impress the jury with the idea that his client was sick and not a man they should send to his death.

The flamboyant sixty-one-year-old lawyer had just finished an interview with *Time* in the July 21, 1986, issue, relating how he had taken a hard line the previous year on legal ethics which had netted him a short jail stay. This involved Rubin's desire to quit the defense of Russell Sanborn, a plumber accused of fatally stabbing an eighteen-year-old woman, when the lawyer learned on the eve of the trial that his client had been lying. Judge Shapiro held Rubin in criminal con-

tempt of court when he refused to continue
to represent Sanborn. Rubin was sentenced
to thirty days in jail as punishment. The lawyer arranged for a habeas corpus petition to
be filed with the Florida Supreme Court and
was promptly released on his own recog-
nizance.

Throughout his career, Ellis Rubin had
made headlines. In 1977, in Miami, he un-
successfully sought an acquittal for teenage
killer Ronald Zamora on the grounds that
"subliminal TV intoxication" had diminished his client's sense of right and wrong.
He had defended Watergate burglars and
championed the cause of Cuban refugees.
Now he was involved once again with an unusual defense in an unusual case.

When Rubin accepted the state's low fee
to represent Long, it was obviously for
"show" and not for "dough."

"We took the case because it's a chal-
lenge," Rubin told reporters, adding that the
case could provide valuable insight in future
textbooks. "Bobby Joe Long is going to become a classic," Rubin promised.

The jury was told that evidence would
show that Long had been exposed to pornography from early childhood, sleeping
with his mother until age thirteen, watching
her engage in sexual relations with other
men, and knowing that she'd once been
raped by her ex-husband, his father. Rubin

contended that the result was Long's perverse adult sexual life. The defense also stated that when Long's breasts began to enlarge at puberty, the malady and resulting corrective surgery left more than just physical scars. Finally, they represented the history of brain damage and doctors' reports supporting the contention that Long was predisposed to commit murder because of forces beyond his control.

This strategy made all of the gory and gruesome pictures, even confessions, part of the defense. The Edwin Meese Pornography Commission concluded the previous week that "The available evidence supports the hypothesis that substantial exposure to sexually violent materials bears a causal relationship to antisocial acts of sexual violence." In 1982 the National Institute of Mental Health concluded there was overwhelming evidence linking television violence and aggression. As always, Rubin was crafting a defense to fit the facts of the case. He linked these current expert opinions to Long's life history.

The local media went to other experts seeking opinions on the unique Rubin defense. Alan Dershowitz of Harvard Law School, himself a much-publicized lawyer, reacted critically. "If this is Ellis Rubin's notion of truth, he has a very, very strange notion. I think it is a ridiculous defense," he added, "an insult to the jury."

The confident Rubin replied, "If Professor Dershowitz is telling you that no link exists, then he should have his own brain examined, not by the Meese Commission but by a lunacy commission."

The media, Alan Dershowitz, and the public all played Rubin's game. The debate shifted from whether Long had done it to why he had done it. The defense knew they had to convince at least six jurors to recommend life because a six-to-six tie of the twelve jurors was a recommendation of life. Unfortunately for Long, the jury was unmoved and eventually voted eleven-to-one for death in the electric chair.

The sentencing trial had opened Wednesday in a routine manner. Michael L. Benito told the jurors that the state would prove four of nine possible reasons for imposing the death penalty under Florida law. He used only a few witnesses to establish the facts of the Simms murder.

Michelle Simms was found with her throat slashed, her head beaten, and a rope around her neck. Autopsy confirmed that any of the three types of assaults would have killed her. This made the crime especially "heinous, atrocious, or cruel," as well as "cold, calculated, and premeditated," two of the aggravating factors under Florida law. It was committed with another violent felony, kidnapping, and by a person with several prior felonies. Each was an aggravating factor in favor of the death sentence. The state rested its case Wednesday afternoon.

After hearing the lengthy Rubin defense, the jury made its recommendation to Judge Griffin. They obviously preferred the state's argument.

Judge Griffin spoke at length about Long's serious mental and emotional problems. These factors did not remove his capacity to appreciate the criminality of his conduct. Therefore, the court found that the four aggravating circumstances proved far outweighed the two mitigating circumstances established. The judge then announced the death sentence for the murder of Michelle Denise Simms on July 25, 1986.

Long now had two death sentences and numerous life sentences with no possible parole for fifty years.

One feature of the Rubin defense strategy was that it burnt all of the defensive bridges. Long's confessions of guilt in his plea bargain had started the process, but this defense had sealed the argument. Long had killed ten women, confessed, and been found guilty.

Referring to the tenth victim, Artis Wick, Benito explained that police suspected Long of another murder but could not prove it. To solve the case, Benito had made a deal with Long's attorney at the time. The state agreed that Long, already guilty of nine murders, would not be charged with the tenth murder if he confessed.

It was revealed that Artis Wick, a green-eyed blonde, had arrived in Tampa four months before her death. She'd hitchhiked there from a small town in Indiana. At noon on March 27, 1984, she had left her apartment to get a pack of cigarettes, and nine months later her badly decomposed body was found in a creek bed off Ponderosa Street in the Sundance area.

After Long's confession to her murder was announced publically, HCSO called Wick's parents, who had not heard from her for more than two years. They had talked to Artis the same day she'd disappeared, which was only one week before she planned to marry.

"She was very excited about her wedding," Mrs. Wick said. When they heard nothing further, they feared the worst. The news of her death ended the long wait. "It was so horrible. We'll never know why someone had to kill her."

A logical outgrowth of this extraordinary sentencing hearing was the appearance of a CBS television crew in court. Long was captured on camera entering court, spitting at the camera, hearing the verdict, and leaving court. In an interview taped on November 25, 1986, Long willingly and publically confessed again to the murders. He told the news crew and television audience how the pickups, rapes, and murders were as easy as A, B, C, D. The report was shown on national television on December 12, 1986, and shown again as part of a documentary on serial killers and task force operations. This second show on CNN contrasted the success of the Tampa task force with the failure of the Green River task force.

This public accounting of the Long murders, task force apprehension, and his conviction seemed like a fitting end to a remarkable case. Long was returned to Florida State Prison's Death Row. This case was, however, far from over, and years of appeals remained.

Twenty-four

Every death sentence in the State of Florida is automatically appealed directly to the Florida Supreme Court. The purpose is to examine trial records and rule on possible errors by judges. Legal rulings on evidence, objections, and the court's findings in support of the death sentence are all thoroughly examined.

Long's conviction and death sentence in the Virginia Johnson case were appealed as soon as the trial and sentencing phase ended on April 27, 1985. Bobby Joe Long was represented by James M. Moorman, tenth judicial circuit public defender, and W. C. (Bill) McLain, chief of capital appeals in the public defender's office.

In direct appeals, few convictions are reversed or vacated. Death sentences are more often returned for rehearing. Ten challenges were raised to Long's conviction and sentence. The Florida Supreme Court addressed only the confession issue, since it was so significant.

Bill McLain is a tall, good-looking blond man who has a commanding presence when he addresses the court. He is so eloquent in his articulate oral arguments that other lawyers often stop by to listen to him.

In this case his arguments were overwhelming. He traced how the U.S. Supreme Court and the Florida Supreme Court in a series of decisions had defined the limits of permitted questioning by police once the accused mentions an attorney. These limits were violated in obtaining Long's confession and the law clearly supported the appeal and the future suppression of the confession. McLain argued that the guideline was specific. Once Long had said in his interrogation, "I think I might need an attorney," the police officers were on notice. The only permissible questioning after that would have been to clarify Long's request for counsel.

The confession tape and testimony were clear. The task force interrogators did not attempt to clarify Long's request for counsel. Instead, they continued to interrogate Long to obtain the eventual confession.

On November 12, 1987, the Florida Supreme Court voted unanimously to vacate Long's confession and death sentence in the Virginia Johnson murder. The court ordered a new trial with Long's confession suppressed.

* * *

The Florida Supreme Court decision complicated Long's subsequent prosecution.
Long's task force confessions could no longer
be used for his conviction. Partly because of
the Johnson death sentence, now vacated,
Long had entered the plea agreement in the
Hillsborough County murders. Part of the
plea agreement was that the guilty plea
(which is a confession in court) and convictions could not be used as aggravating factors
in subsequent cases. When the agreement
was written, it referred to the Simms sentencing phase. These questions arose: were
all of the Hillsborough murder confessions
and convictions barred in the new Johnson
trial and sentencing? What status did the
television confessions have? If Long's confession had been suppressed, would he have
agreed to a plea bargain? Without the
Johnson conviction and death sentence,
would Long have received the death sentence
in the Simms murder? This last question was
soon answered. Other parts of the legal puz-
zle took longer to untangle.

Ellis Rubin had immediately appealed the
Simms conviction and sentence. The Florida
Supreme Court ruled on this appeal on June
30, 1988. They held that the suppression of
Long's original task force confession did not
allow Long to set aside his plea agreement.

Obviously, Long's plea agreement was a poor decision once the original confession was thrown out. The Florida Supreme Court ruled that the plea agreement was entered by Long voluntarily after consultation with competent counsel. He was offered an opportunity to withdraw the plea agreement, considered it for twenty-four hours, and entered the agreement knowing that it could not be appealed. Therefore the convictions in all of the cases, including Simms, were affirmed.

The Virginia Johnson conviction and death sentence were used as an aggravating factor in the Simms sentencing hearing. The four aggravating circumstances outnumbered and outweighed the two mitigating factors. Since the Supreme Court could not predict that the jury and judge would reach the same decision without the Johnson verdict, the court concluded that Long deserved a new sentencing hearing before another jury.

Commenting on this new sentencing hearing order, assistant state attorney Benito observed, "Long and his attorney detailed the ten murders in court, including the Virginia Johnson murder. The Pasco County verdict reversal therefore was harmless error and it did not affect the sentence. It is like the Supreme Court did not read the transcript."

This Supreme Court decision meant that Long currently had no death sentences and his only current conviction where he could receive death was the Simms plea-agreement conviction. Over three and a half years after Long's capture, he was still not sentenced to die, and his murder trials had a long way to go.

The Virginia Johnson retrial was begun almost immediately. Pretrial hearings were held on August 18, 1988, and October 24, 1988. In these hearings the court ruled that Phillip Van Allen, prosecutor, would be allowed to introduce Williams Rule evidence, which is the evidence of similar crimes. Details of the murders of Lana Long, Michelle Simms, Karen Dinsfriend, and Kim Swann were allowed to be presented. The court ruled that the McVey rape could not be presented under Williams Rule because it was not similar. The state attorneys stated that McVey would not be used as a "criminal episode" but would be used to show how Long had been arrested. Assistant Public Defender Robert McClure objected strenuously throughout these rulings, setting the stage for future appeals.

After an unsuccessful attempt to empanel a jury in Pasco County, a change of venue was granted. The retrial of Long for the murder of Virginia Johnson was begun on November 1, 1988, in Fort Myers, Florida.

The defense counsel moved for a mistrial after the prosecutor's opening statement, when details of the McVey rape and abduction were recounted. The defense contended that this violated Williams Rule.

This incident typified the whole trial, in which both prosecution and defense were unsure what information from which Long cases could be used. The prosecution presented only four hours of testimony establishing the Johnson murder facts: discovery, identification, and hair and fiber ties to Long's vehicle.

In contrast, evidence about other Long cases was introduced over the next three days. The jury was instructed that the other crime evidence could be considered only to prove motive, plan, and identity. During each step, the defense team objected. They charged that the McVey testimony and the CBS videotape were becoming the main feature of the case, and that none of this was evidence in the Virginia Johnson murder.

The CBS News videotape showed about one minute of Victoria Corderi's one-and-a-half-hour interview. The following statements given by Bobby Joe Long were said at different points in the interview but were edited as one continual piece.

In the revealing interview, Long said, "I don't know, but all in all I must have destroyed about a hundred people . . . it was like A, B, C, D. I'd pull over, they'd get in. I'd drive a little ways, stop, pull out a knife, a gun, whatever, tie them up, and take them out. That would be it . . . and the worst thing is, I don't understand why. I don't understand why.

"I figured it was so obvious there's something wrong with me that when they did catch me, that they would fix me," he concluded.

In his closing argument, assistant state attorney Van Allen established a pattern between the four Long murders presented and the Johnson death. He closed by saying, "We have shown you that every time a hooker gets together with Bobby Joe Long she dies by strangulation."

Assistant Public Defender Robert McClure countered that the prosecutors had not proved that Virginia Johnson was killed in Pasco County or that her death was premeditated. McClure urged the jury, "You have to put aside your hatred in this case and apply the law."

In the second Virginia Johnson trial, the jury spent only sixty-three minutes finding Long guilty of strangling Johnson. As the verdict was announced, Long stood with his hands in his pockets and rolled his head from side to side.

A week later, on November 8, 1988, the penalty phase was held and Long was again sentenced to death. The defense had strong grounds for appeal. No one doubted that

Long had murdered Johnson. It was simply very difficult to present the case in court.

Prior to the second Johnson trial, CBS Evening News fought turning over the entire Long interview in Florida's Second District Court of Appeals in Lakeland. When the court ruled that defense lawyers were entitled to certain outtakes, the network agreed to surrender thirteen minutes of tape.

Long told CBS that he'd raped and murdered without thinking of the consequences. "To tell you the truth, I never considered the electric chair," he said. Long estimated that he had committed about a hundred rapes and ten murders without any clear reason.

"I don't know why," he offered sheepishly. He remembered driving home after the first rape thinking that he must be nuts.

Long said only one of his early victims had ever come to any harm, and that was a woman who'd grabbed the blade of a knife he'd used to threaten her. Unbelievably, he stated, "I tried to be as gentle as I could."

This approach changed completely when Long, then an unemployed X-ray technician, broke up with a nurse he had dated. She was different in that she was a nice, religious woman whom Long believed would turn his life around.

First Long would say that he did not blame anyone other than himself for his ac-

tions, but in the next moment, he observed,
"My former girlfriend got me in the state of
mind where I was going to shoot people or
had to get in fights."

Long related that the first of the Tampa
Bay murders in 1984 had occurred after he'd
had a few drinks at a topless bar.

"I'm not a drinker," he remarked, "so two
or three drinks hit me." He still insisted that
he'd had no plan to kill when he'd picked
up Lana Long.

Long said he had spotted the woman walking down the street wearing a miniskirt, tube
top, beret, and high heels. She told him she
was going to a bar, so he agreed to give her
a ride. Just before they arrived, however, he
turned off the street and drove to a rural
area.

"I don't know what it was about this girl,
but it was very violent," he recalled. "After
that it was just like clockwork."

Long never looked directly at the camera
during the interview. He related the horrific
tale without emotion or remorse. The only
sign of humanity arose as he described the
abduction of seventeen-year-old Lisa McVey.
He grabbed the girl from her bicycle as she
rode home from work late at night. Afterward, he raped her repeatedly during a
twenty-six-hour orgy at his apartment.

"This wasn't some streetwalker," he em-
phasized. "This was a young girl on her way

home from a doughnut shop. Things were just starting to come into my mind involving women I know. That [incident] was a real clear sign that I was losing control. Let's face it, that's insane," he concluded, as if discussing the actions of someone else.

Commenting on Lisa McVey, Long said, "I understand that she would like to see me in the electric chair, and I can't blame her. I might feel the same way."

Later in the interview, Long feigned regret. "I thought about [the victims] a lot. I think it's really just sad what happened to them. There was no pleasure in any of this stuff." Shortly thereafter, the real Bobby Joe reappeared. He laughed and said that he'd murdered so impulsively that once he'd popped a TV dinner into the oven, stepped out for some milk, and killed a woman before returning. "My apartment almost burned down by the time I got back," he chuckled.

It was almost four years before the Florida Supreme Court announced their decision in the Johnson retrial. The conviction and sentence were reversed and remanded for a second time in their October 15, 1992, decision. The court ruled that once the state introduced statements made in a videotaped interview, the defendant was entitled to have the entire interview placed in evidence. The court also ruled that evidence of other murders under the plea agreement were not admissible.

In their detailed opinion, the court answered many of the legal questions complicating the Long case. Their conclusion: "At a new trial the CBS interview may be admitted into evidence provided the entire videotape is available for viewing by the jury. Second, evidence of the murders to which Long entered guilty pleas in the Hillsborough County plea agreement may not be admitted under the circumstances of this case. Third, testimony concerning the McVey incident may be admitted to identify Long in the case so long as the details of Long's treatment of McVey in his apartment and his subsequent plea of guilty in that case are excluded. Finally, evidence of the Hillsborough County guilty pleas and convictions resulting from Long's plea agreement may not be admitted as aggravating factors given the terms of the plea agreement." The lines of conduct for the third Virginia Johnson murder trial were somewhat defined.

On the same day, October 15, 1992, the Florida Supreme Court upheld the death sentence in the second Michelle Simms penalty-phase proceeding. This hearing had been moved from Hillsborough County to Daytona Beach to escape the intense publicity on the west coast of Florida. It was held in the Volusia

County Courthouse Annex, which sits on City Island in the Halifax River. It was in room 5 on the second floor of the building. In making his decision to move the sentencing phase, Judge Richard A. Lazzara, Jr., was heavily influenced by the large number of letters from Tampa area attorneys that stated that in their opinion, pretrial publicity would make a fair trial extremely difficult in Hillsborough County.

When Long had tried to delay the hearing, claiming insufficient time to prepare his defense, Benito snapped, "How much time did you give Michelle Simms for her defense?" Long's reply was a muffled, "Fuck you."

Ellis Rubin handled the first Simms sentencing phase hearing and appeal only. The second Simms sentencing defense attorney was Robert Fraser from the public defender's office. This defense strategy was more standard.

The defense's case included new testimony not previously presented. Long's mother testified that she was married to the man who had taught Bobby Joe the electrical trade and that he had become a father figure to him. She later determined that the man was already married and had the marriage annulled, which she believed hurt her son. To complicate matters further, at this time she began living with a man Bobby Joe despised.

Five head injuries to Long, all resulting in

periods of unconsciousness, were documented. Long's ex-wife, Cynthia Bartlet, testified that the last of these accidents had resulted in a personality change. Long now suffered from violent mood changes and had a significantly increased sex drive. Cynthia was permitted to testify on videotape at her doctor's request. She detailed that when twelve-year-old Bobby Joe had shared a bed with his mother, she would bring home male guests for the night and send the boy to a living room couch.

Dr. John Money, of Johns Hopkins School of Medicine, testified that Long had a brain disorder, "sexual sadism," which caused his criminal behavior. Long was diagnosed as having temporal lobe epilepsy which caused extreme highs or depression instead of seizures. This often accompanied sexual sadism. Dr. Money testified that sexual sadists become sexually aroused by inflicting pain, but that such an individual is also capable of having sex as a loving act. He stated that Long's description of his feelings during the murder of Simms indicated that he was in an altered state of consciousness brought on by the temporal lobe epilepsy.

Dr. Berland believed that Long had been under the influence of an extreme mental or emotional disturbance and had killed Simms in a fit of rage. The state had Dr. Sprehe testify in rebuttal. Long told Sprehe that he had used a rope and a piece of wood and had had a knife with him when he'd killed Simms. He quoted Long as saying he'd killed Simms to "eliminate a witness," but that he would not have killed her if a policeman had been standing there. Dr. Sprehe concluded that Long had had the capacity to appreciate the criminality of his conduct and his ability to conform to the law had not been impaired.

It is interesting to note that the insanity defense was never used by Long's defense. In four trials and sentencing phases no jury or judge seemed to believe that Long was mentally impaired.

At the conclusion of the hearing, Judge Richard A. Lazzara, Jr., found four aggravating circumstances in favor of the death penalty and two mitigating factors against death. The jury had recommended unanimously that Long receive the death sentence. The two felonies where Long was previously convicted using violence replaced the Johnson case as an aggravating factor.

As the handcuffed Long exited the courtroom and was escorted across the hall to the waiting van, a cameraman asked for a final comment. Long smiled at the camera as a policeman held the door open for him and said, "The jurors shouldn't have been so upset."

After the sentencing hearing, Long wrote

Judge Lazzara several letters strongly criticizing his lawyer, Robert Fraser. Long told the judge that he had filed a grievance with the Florida bar concerning his legal representation.

The Florida Supreme Court denied a motion for rehearing in the Simms conviction and death sentences on January 26, 1993. The direct appeal in the Simms case was complete. The collateral appeals were still to come, but they had to be filed within one year of the case being final. In this phase new legal counsel was provided from the Capital Collateral Representative's Office for indigents such as Bobby Joe Long. The third Virginia Johnson murder trial was still to come.

Twenty-five

Ten years after the strangulation death of Virginia Johnson, Bobby Joe Long was, for the third time, being tried for her murder. This time the trial was being held in the new Marion County Judicial Center in Ocala after an effort to seat a jury in Pasco County had failed. Here the jury selection had been promptly made on February 1, 1994, and the sparsely attended trial began. There was no national coverage this time, and no video cameras; there were few reporters at all. Even the use of hand-held tape recorders was denied. There was a sense of antipublicity paranoia. Security remained acute, with guards at all entrances and locked doors when the session began.

Courtroom 4-C, in which the trial was held, is a small room that bears a striking resemblance to a theater. The stage counterpart is round with twelve separate bright light panels overhead. Pasco-Pinellas Circuit Court Judge Charles W. Cope was prominently seated near the top of the circle facing a four-man, eight-woman jury on his right. To his immediate right was the witness stand, and behind that were doors that all used to make their entrances. Their backs to spectators, but center stage with the jury on their left, sat assistant state attorneys Phillip Van Allen and James Hellison. To their right, beside a door where he had entered from his holding cell, sat Bobby Joe Long, flanked by assistant public defenders William Eble and Laurie Chane. Extending in front of this judicial sphere were individual upholstered theater-style armchairs, six rows and six seats across on either side. These were designed to provide seventy-two people with comfortable viewing, but ironically, no more than possibly a dozen at one time were ever present.

James Hellison, conservative looking in wire-rimmed glasses and a dark suit, gave impressive opening remarks to the jury. He said that concerning Virginia Johnson, the state would determine whether the defendant had committed first-degree murder. When he mentioned the abduction of Lisa McVey, Elbe popped up, one of numerous times throughout the trial, to request a conference with the judge. Afterward Hellison continued by referring to Long's television interview, in which he admitted to nine murders including Johnson's, saying that the murders were as simple as A, B, C, and D.

Hellison said he would like to add M for murder.

Assistant public defender Eble rose to address the jury. He is a confident attorney, physically small and well tailored. On the little finger of each hand he wore a gold ring. He was unusually fair skinned for a Floridian and his light sandy-colored hair was meticulously styled. His movements seemed studied and deliberate as he spoke. He told the jury that although Long had done some bad things, he wanted them to keep an open mind in this case. He referred to the discovery of Johnson's decomposed body and questioned the medical examiner's findings. Could Johnson have died of a drug overdose or other cause? He added that DNA was not used in this case and the hair evidence was not conclusive. "Actually," he said, "you can't be certain where Johnson died."

A long list of witnesses were interviewed again, including the Tampa man in whose house Johnson had stayed, the women who had found her body, plus the law enforcement people who had been active in the case. Some of the witnesses could not recall their exact testimony of 1985 and seemed perturbed to be asked to do so. Long seemed almost bored with the proceedings and sat much of the time with his arms folded over his blue suit. Sometimes he spoke briefly with Laurie Chane, who sat amiably beside him. He only moved to cast a dark stare at anyone leaving or entering the courtroom.

Although the defense had tried to restrain it, a shapely Lisa McVey took the stand on the third day of the trial. She was very emotional and continually wiped away tears. During the ten years since her kidnapping, she had matured into a beautiful woman who apparently had been unable to erase the trauma of her ordeal. Nervously she stroked her long, curly brown hair as she responded to questions. She avoided looking at Long, who watched her intently.

Elbe was frustrated when McVey went through the details of her abduction and rape. He demanded to know how she could identify Long when she had been blindfolded. She lowered her head, weeping quietly, and said she just knew. When it was revealed that she had been offered a movie deal in 1985, Elbe asked for a mistrial in order to study the contract. This was denied. Continuing his interrogation, Elbe's frustration grew and he and the prosecution again conferred with the judge. Calmly, the judge spoke aloud to Elbe, saying, "If you do not go over the line, I'll control the court."

Elbe asked more about the movie prospects. McVey said that she had been approached by John Eastman in 1985 and had been given $1500, but she had heard nothing further until last year. She said Eastman had been vague about money and her actual participation in his project. She had, however, appeared on two talk shows in the Tampa area, but had received no pay. She said she simply wanted others to know of her story.

Detective Polly Goethe Horn took the stand. She was plainly dressed in black slacks and appeared very composed. She said that she was with the Tampa police department and had also been approached in 1985 to help John Eastman make a movie. She said she gave him her interviews, and she believed that he had also interviewed McVey. The detective remarked that she had an agreement with Eastman and had received about $1000 from him in 1985 or 1986. Eastman had called her again in 1993 to say that he was close to final arrangements. Elbe shook his head. How many other law enforcement officials received money from Eastman and had participated in his project? he asked. The detective said she knew of no others.

Late in the afternoon, FBI special agent Michael Malone was sworn in, but then he was immediately dismissed while Elbe and Van Allen conferred with the judge for a lengthy six minutes. After being called back again to the stand, Malone gave detailed responses to Van Allen's questions but addressed all his remarks directly to the jury. FBI personnel standards have been rigidly defined. Generally, the FBI look is to be tall, alert, with healthy looks, tailored dark suit that blends in, and good leather shoes. Malone looked FBI.

He was quickly established by the prosecution as a hair and fiber expert who teaches throughout the country. He told about his lab's role in identifying the murderer through matching Johnson's hair with two treated blond hairs from Long's car. In the scraping room he studied the vacuumed sweepings from Long's car through a stereoscope. Any hair located was mounted, and he compared the known to the unknown for a match. He used three different microscopes to look at the root and tip from which he could determine the person's race, which area of the body it had come from, and whether or not the hair had been forcibly removed. Next he used a higher-powered 400 to determine the size, shape, and color pigment. "This is not a fingerprint," he said, "but it's very identifiable."

Looking for fibers, he located a red lustrous trilobal nylon fiber, analyzed its dye (manufacturers do not duplicate dyes but patent them), and determined it to be a carpet fiber. Samples involving Long's hair were found. Now he had a double transfer of hair and fiber.

These fiber samples and Long's hair were also found on Lisa McVey's clothing. As he had done several times before, Malone covered each detail in the evidence gathering process. This trace evidence was a key ingredient in linking Long to the murder of Virginia Johnson. It was even more important now that Long's original confession had been suppressed.

Another dramatic period in the trial came when a 1986 videotaped interview with Long was played. At the time of this interview, Long had pleaded guilty to eight murders in Hillsborough County and the Pasco jury had convicted him of Virginia Johnson's murder. He told of picking up his victims, many of whom were prostitutes, tying them up, and killing them in the now familiar A, B, C, D method.

Van Allen said that it was in this manner that Long had killed Johnson sometime in late October or early November, 1984.

"If he didn't intend to kill, all he had to do was let go," Van Allen stated in his closing arguments on Saturday.

The jury deliberated nearly three hours and came back with a verdict of guilty. They had based this verdict on the strength of the hair and fiber evidence and the videotaped interview.

When the conviction of first-degree murder was read by the court clerk, Bobby Joe

Long nonchalantly poured himself a glass of water. By now the guilty verdict was the expected outcome.

Twenty-six

The FBI law enforcement bulletin printed a two-part article in 1987 entitled "A Study in Cooperation" with thirteen pages devoted to the Bobby Joe Long case. Details of the murders, task force investigation, and FBI participation were covered, as were Long's apprehension, capture, and conviction.

This was an early positive example of how knowledgeable law enforcement officers from multiple agencies could work together in a task force. This was the first example of FBI forensics helping local law enforcement agencies identify and capture an active serial killer. Currently, visitors to the FBI forensics lab are still given a one-hour slide briefing on the Long case as an example of what hair and fiber evidence can accomplish.

The Florida Department of Law Enforcement considers Bobby Joe Long to be Florida's first real serial killer. Ted Bundy, Gerald Stano, and others *confessed* to serial murders. Long was stopped at the height of his killing spree, and law enforcement personnel tied ten murder cases to him, together with hard evidence that stood up in court.

Det. Lee Baker, HCSO, interviewed both Stano and Long. "In the Stano case there were only his confessions, no other evidence," Baker said. "We chose not to prosecute. In the Long case, we caught him with good police work and evidence that tied him to each victim."

Prof. Steven Egger, a criminologist from Sangamon State University, observed, "The Long case is a good example, in terms of the investigation, of what a serial murder investigation should be. At least it's an excellent example of cooperation between local law enforcement and federal authorities."

Long grotesquely murdered women, then left them prominently displayed so their discovery could tell the tale of tortured death. The media, reporting these deaths in dramatic detail, created absolute fear throughout the area's population of two million. Not only strippers and prostitutes felt threatened, but women throughout the entire metropolitan area did as well.

After the reported murders were linked, media coverage was accelerated. Early stories were repeated and expanded with photographs, map locations, and new interviews.

The public was exposed to, and gripped by, this for almost a year. Even after Long's arrest, the subsequent trials kept him constantly in the news for over two years. Even ten years after his capture, any news about the progress of his case is highly publicized and followed with interest.

Currently, Bobby Joe Long has been found guilty of murder and sentenced to die three times in the Virginia Johnson murder and twice in the Michelle Simms case. This is in addition to the eight sentences of life in prison with no consideration of parole for fifty years.

Long has confessed explicitly to the murders first to the police, then to a national television interviewer, a third time in court with his guilty plea bargains, and also to inmates in jail. He allowed his attorney, Ellis Rubin, to use these ten murder confessions as a fact in his insanity defense in the Simms sentencing hearing. The FBI used hair, fiber, and chemical evidence to link Long to the victims, plus tire marks from his car to tie him to the murder scenes. The large knife which Long used in some murders was recovered at his house.

Some ask why this man is still alive after ten years. There are many answers. The Long case was stuck in the first phase for ten years. The Florida Supreme Court reversed the convictions and sentences twice in the Johnson case and once in the Simms case. The trials that followed, and the resulting death sentences, were appealed again and again. By definition, law enforcement officers desperately want to capture suspects, and prosecutors want convictions in high-profile cases.

In the Long interrogation, when law enforcement officers ignored Long's casual remark "I guess I need an attorney," the whole serial murder confession that followed was inadmissible. Any person reading the transcript could expect the defense to appeal on this point. Yet the interrogation continued though the confession and the Virginia Johnson case went to trial based on this tainted confession. This fact shows how desperate the task force was to stop the serial killer, and how much the prosecutor wanted to get a quick conviction. They were under tremendous pressure from the public, which was fervently following the apprehension and conviction of the killer. Appellate decisions two or three years later directing retrials and declaring confessions inadmissible are not considered significant by the public. Blame is usually assigned to a liberal court or to laws which favor criminals, but they note that the serial killer is in fact still in jail.

In the reversal of the second Virginia

Johnson trial and the first Michelle Simms sentencing trial, Williams Rule was often discussed. This rule originated in a 1959 serial rapist case. In the trial of the first rape, evidence of other similar, but untried rape cases was introduced by the state. The case was affirmed on appeal, and the rule, later codified by statute, was created that limits evidence of acts, crimes, or wrongs that prove identity, lack of consent, or lack of mistake. The court always assumes that the admission of Williams Rule evidence is prejudicial.

Prosecutors are faced with the difficult task of using other case evidence while staying within the evidence rules allowed. In the Virginia Johnson second trial, the prosecutor could not use Long's confession. When he used McVey under Williams Rule, he was trying to prove identity and lack of mistake and show a pattern. Often witnesses, like McVey, from other similar cases will volunteer answers in their testimony that violate the Williams Rule. Even lawyers and judges find difficulty interpreting the Williams Rule.

How will the Long case proceed? After the Florida Supreme Court upheld the Simms death sentence in January, 1993, the defense asked the United States Supreme Court to accept the case. On October 4, 1993, the high court declined to hear the case. Pursuant to the Florida Rules of Criminal Procedure, Long has one year to file his collateral appeal.

The Florida Capital Collateral Representatives have filed motions in Long's behalf under Florida Rule of Criminal Procedure 3.850 for post-conviction relief. These collateral claims address issues outside the trial record such as ineffective assistance of counsel and involuntary pleas. The claims are originated in the state trial court of origin.

On December 27, 1994, assistant capital collateral representative Terri Backhus filed the first motion to vacate judgment and sentence in Bobby Joe Long's case. It was filed in the circuit court in Hillsborough County, where the case began ten years ago.

Prisoners sentenced to death have the additional benefit of an attorney's assistance when mounting this collateral attack. Ordinary lifers and other prisoners are not usually favored with an attorney to help them at this stage of the appeals process. As a result, this rule of criminal procedure, 3.850, is written so that a person untrained in the law can fill out the motion and present it to the court. Felons toil in the prison library, scrawling out new facts they hope will provide the keys to freedom. The instructions on the model form clearly state: "You must allege facts. The motion will not be accepted by the Court if grounds are not supported by the facts."

The thirty-three-page motion filed by CCR on Long's behalf does not present any material facts which uniquely apply to Long and the Simms case. There are no specific assaults upon either Mr. O'Connor or Mr. Rubin. The court files, presumably in the possession of Long's current counsels, includes the letters written by Bobby Joe to Judge Lazzara bitterly complaining about the representation he received from Mr. O'Connor. The absence of key defense experts like Dr. Morrison is well documented, yet not cited as a reason to vacate the judgment and sentence. Facts exist in the record to support claims that the plea agreement was not voluntarily entered into with a full understanding of all of the rights Long was waiving, yet these claims are not included in CCR's motion. The plea is a dilatory effort, presented to cause delay and buy time.

In the introduction to the motion, Long's current counsels confess that they are unable to properly represent Long due to budget and time constraints. CCR's motion points to counsel's caseload, which it claims makes it impossible to properly investigate and present Long's post-conviction claims. They allege that the motion is incomplete due to the failure of the various state agencies to comply with public records requests. The records desired, required, or missing are not identified, just repeatedly referred to as the reason for having no factual allegations to support claim after claim.

The motion is standard in the day of word processing, a cut-and-paste effort with lackluster boilerplate claims. In this motion, CCR presents conclusory allegations without supporting facts. For instance, in claim two, they allege, "Mr. Long's plea was not voluntary. Mr. Long's plea was not knowingly and intelligently made." No mention of how or why is evident. "Mr. Long cannot adequately plead this claim until he receives full compliance with all of his requests for records, documents, files, and other evidence." What documents, records, and files? The motion contains several requests to amend the motion as information is available and to extend the time to file as necessary to support the twenty-five claims presented.

These claims include standard attacks on Florida's death penalty statute based in part on recent U.S. Supreme Court decisions. Even though the search of Long's car and apartment was pursuant to a warrant, and even though he later waived these rights, Long's attorneys now claim that his fourth amendment rights were violated. Even though the confession is currently suppressed, they claim that his fifth and sixth amendment rights to be free from continued custodial interrogation without benefit of an attorney were violated. Death is cruel and unusual, alleges the motion, despite several court decisions upholding the sentence. The most surprising claim is the last offering: "Mr. Long is innocent and the State failed to present sufficient evidence to prove Mr. Long was guilty as charged . . ." Long admitted the charges in court with his guilty plea. His requested attorney, Ellis Rubin, used his crimes as evidence claiming that Bobby Joe needed medical treatment for mental disorders. He confessed again to news reporters and various interviewers. Yet now CCR claims that no rational jury could find Mr. Long guilty of premeditated murder beyond a reasonable doubt.

This phase of the Long appeal will probably last another three to five years. After this, another ten years or so will be used raising issues in federal courts, claiming a violation of federal rights that were denied in state courts. Long could possibly be in jail a total of twenty-five years while appeals are exhausted before his death sentence is enforced.

By then, Michelle Simms could have been a grandmother.

Twenty-seven

Restructuring our criminal justice system is an ever-popular issue with political aspirants, and the public demands it whenever there is a high-profile murder case. Every election year, national and state candidates for office strongly respond to voter demand to reduce crime, keep people who are convicted of serious crimes in jail, and shorten the appeals process, especially in capital cases. Elected representatives seem sincere, but for one reason or another, laws to make these changes are not enacted.

The War on Crime and the War on Drugs fell short of their stated goals. Convicted murderers sit on Death Row for decades as Congressional response is incomplete and ineffective. In 1994, the much-touted crime bill added over fifty federal crimes to the list of potential death penalty cases, but only a small fraction of people sentenced to death will actually be executed. The federal government will not use their new capital punishment law in this century; it will be nearly impossible to execute someone under this law for many years. The underlying problem with capital punishment is the delay between imposition and execution of sentence.

The prosecutor in the Long case summed up this frustration: "One of my biggest peeves about working as a prosecutor and getting these death penalties," remarked Mike Benito, "is that they go on ten, eleven, twelve years, and it's pathetic. Think about this. Theodore Bundy killed the girl, Kimberly Leech, when she was twelve years old and they executed Bundy after about ten or eleven years. . . . How can convicted killers stay alive for so many years? It's beyond me, but that's the way the system works. . . . As the guys on Death Row are appealing, sometimes the law changes and they'll take advantage of that. If you can wait long enough on Death Row, something's going to happen to your case where you may eventually get another hearing. . . .

"At one time I had maybe thirteen or fourteen guys on Death Row. The first guy I put there was named Michael Squires, and that was March of 1982. He was on Death Row for twelve years and died there August 1993 of a respiratory illness."

The public, the executive branch, and the Congress are all interested in shortening the appeals process, but there are large areas of delay which are unresolved. There is *no* time limit on the length of time judges may take before making a decision. Federal appellate courts are notoriously slow. They can add ten years to the life of a death-sentenced inmate.

In our legal system, the judiciary imposes sentences, but the executive branch carries them out. A governor must sign a death warrant and they do not sign all that are presented to them. The failure to sign death warrants may be a cause for further delay.

Defense attorneys also waste time by requesting and receiving numerous delays. Courts should honor a defendant's constitutional rights, but when a defense attorney repeatedly tries to buy time by filing claims, making delays which prove fruitless, or employing improper tactics, the attorney should be penalized.

The problems with capital punishment in America may be more difficult to solve than signing more warrants and finding a few attorneys in contempt of court for delaying tactics. A good measure of the chaos is the predictable result of the U.S. Supreme Court's 1972 decision in *Furman v. Georgia*. The defense argued that all death penalty statutes were unconstitutional because they resulted in arbitrary and capricious imposition of the death penalty. As a direct result, the majority of people put to death were poor and members of racial minorities. Robbers were condemned to die, while murderers served short prison terms. This case was a direct assault on capital punishment and is as close as the Supreme Court has ever come to outlawing the practice in America. In a badly fractured decision, each justice had a different view on how the states could execute people without offending their federal constitutional rights. A majority of justices agreed that the eighth amendment did not prohibit death as a cruel and unusual punishment, but beyond that, states were given precious little guidance on how to mend their laws.

In the confusion that followed *Furman,* Florida hastily enacted a new statute that would permit capital punishment and pass constitutional muster. A two-part process was created for jury trials in first-degree murder cases. After the guilt phase, if the defendant was convicted, then the same jury convened to hear evidence in the second phase of the trial. The purpose of this proceeding was to consider whether the appropriate sentence was death, or life in prison. The jury would make a non-binding recommendation to the judge. The statute designed to resolve arbitrary application of the death penalty created as many questions as it resolved.

One aggravating factor that tilts the balance in favor of death is when a murder was especially heinous, atrocious, or cruel, however what may be unbearable suffering to one judge may be inherent in the crime in the eyes of another. Another aggravating factor is when a defendant caused a great risk of death to many persons. How many is many? How great is great?

Mitigating circumstances are no clearer. A defendant's age is to be considered in mitigation. But one judge may find that a sixteen-year-old should pay the ultimate penalty for a murder, while another judge may be reluctant to impose death on a person "only" nineteen or twenty. How many convictions are permissible before a defendant has a "significant" criminal history?

Not only is the task of reviewing death sentences a daunting and nearly impossible task; the playing field is constantly shifting. The state of the law changes during the years and years cases are pending on appeal. Courts decide new cases every day, which change legal standards. Recently, the U.S. Supreme Court issued several important decisions concerning capital punishment and other criminal issues. Some of these cases favor the defendant; other favor the state. But the problem is that new decisions can affect pending cases and cause settled issues to be reopened. Courts hear and rehear the same cases time after time. Will Long's convictions and sentences be changed by new decisions?

No one knows until future appeals are decided in his case.

In the summer of 1994, the U.S. Supreme Court decided that equivocal requests for counsel did not implicate the constitutional safeguards. If a criminal suspect being interrogated does not clearly state that he wants to talk to an attorney, law enforcement officers are not required to cease questioning. Statements like "I think I need an attorney" or "Maybe I should talk to a lawyer" are not enough to trigger constitutional rights. So, if Bobby Joe Long's confession was now introduced in court, federal constitutional law would not require that it be excluded. At another retrial, Long may be faced with a whole new ballgame with new rules.

The U.S. Supreme Court has also called into question several of the statutory aggravating factors in Florida's death penalty statute in a series of decisions in the early 1990s. Other Florida Death Row inmates convinced the high court that the instructions to the jury concerning these statutes were vague and resulted in the unfair imposition of the death sentence. The aggravating factors— that the murder was committed in a cold, calculated, and premeditated manner and that the murder was especially heinous, atrocious, or cruel— are in question. Florida judges found these aggravating factors when sentencing Bobby Joe Long to death. So once again, appellate courts may reverse Long's death sentences for further consideration. Years and years remain before Long exhausts his rights to appellate review.

Friends and relatives of the victims hope this is not the case. In any event, life in the shadow of the gallows may be a fate worse than death, and like all men, eventually Bobby Joe Long is bound to die.

**ORDINARY LIVES DESTROYED BY EXTRAORDINARY HORROR.
FACTS MORE DANGEROUS THAN FICTION.
CAPTURE A PINNACLE TRUE CRIME . . . IF YOU DARE.**

LITTLE GIRL LOST   (593, $4.99)
By Joan Merriam
When Anna Brackett, an elderly woman living alone, allowed two teenage
girls into her home, she never realized that a brutal death awaited her.
Within an hour, Mrs. Brackett would be savagely stabbed twenty-eight
times. Her executioners were Shirley Katherine Wolf, 14, and Cindy Lee
Collier, 15. *Little Girl Lost* examines how two adolescents were driven
through neglect and sexual abuse to commit the ultimate crime.

HUSH, LITTLE BABY   (541, $4.99)
By Jim Carrier
Darci Kayleen Pierce seemed to be the kind of woman you stand next to in
the grocery store. However, Darci was obsessed with the need to be a
mother. She desperately wanted a baby—any baby. On a summer day,
Darci kidnapped a nine-month pregnant woman, strangled her, and performed a makeshift Cesarean section with a car key. In this arresting account, readers will learn how Pierce's tortured fantasy of motherhood
spiralled into a bloody reality.

IN A FATHER'S RAGE   (547, $4.99)
By Raymond Van Over
Dr. Kenneth Z. Taylor promised his third wife Teresa that he would mend
his drug-addictive, violent ways. His vow didn't last. He nearly beat his
bride to death on their honeymoon. This nuptial nightmare worsened
until Taylor killed Teresa after allegedly catching her sexually abusing
their infant son. Claiming to have been driven beyond a father's rage, Taylor was still found guilty of first degree murder. This gripping page-turner
reveals how a marriage made in heaven can become a living hell.

I KNOW MY FIRST NAME IS STEVEN   (563, $4.99)
By Mike Echols
A TV movie was based on this terrifying tale of abduction, child molest-
ing, and brainwashing. Yet, a ray of hope shines through this evil swamp
for Steven Stayner escaped from his captor and testified against the so-
cially distrubed Kenneth Eugene Parnell. For seven years, Steven was
shuttled across California under the assumed name of "Dennis Parnell."
Despite the humiliations and degradations, Steven never lost sight of his
origins or his courage.

RITES OF BURIAL   (611, $4.99)
By Tom Jackman and Troy Cole
Many pundits believe that the atrocious murders and dismemberments
performed by Robert Berdella may have inspired Jeffrey Dahmer. Berdella
stalked and savagely tortured young men; sadistically photographing their
suffering and ritualistically preserving totems from their deaths. Upon his
arrest, police uncovered human skulls, envelopes of teeth, and a partially
decomposed human head. This shocking expose is written by two men
who worked daily on this case.

*Available wherever paperbacks are sold, or order direct from the
Publisher. Send cover price plus 50¢ per copy for mailing and
handling to Penguin USA, P.O. Box 999, c/o Dept. 17109,
Bergenfield, NJ 07621. Residents of New York and Tennessee
must include sales tax. DO NOT SEND CASH.*